Charge to a New Bishop

*"Be to the flock of Christ a shepherd, not a wolf;
feed them, do not devour them. Hold up the weak,
heal the sick, bind up the broken, bring back the lapsed,
and seek the lost."*

The Book of Common Prayer, p. 507

Dedication

This is my personal story, but it is also the story of the amazing renewal and miraculous anointing in a Church that I love, a Church I have nurtured, prayed for, helped strengthen, and wept for as it has largely abandoned its own received teaching. The good news is that God has raised up a faithful alternative.

This book is dedicated to the woman who shared most of its history with me: my wife. partner, playmate, confidante, chief advisor, most incisive critic, greatest encourager, wickedest card player, and very best friend, Karen. Thank you so much for everything.

Endorsements and Comments

What a gift is Bishop John Howe's book to all in Christian ministry! John was one of the most outstanding bishops in the Anglican Communion during my time as Archbishop of Canterbury and his book illustrates why he was such an effective pastor, preacher, and leader. Read it for its wisdom, humor, and experiences but, most of all, read it to grow as a Christian yourself.

George Carey
The 103rd Archbishop of Canterbury, 1991-2002

Bishop John Howe's ministry coincided with the terrible demise of the Episcopal Church, losing more than a million parishioners. This was happening at the same time that the half dozen places that John and Karen did their ministry were growing remarkably. Surely there is a lesson here! If the leadership of the bishops of the Episcopal Church in those days had been one that we see in John, then doubtless the Episcopal Church would have grown by a million, rather than losing by more than a million. John Howe's biography is truly a historical document that is a lesson for us all now.

C. FitzSimons Allison
Twelfth Episcopal Bishop of South Carolina,
Professor of Church History, the University of the South and
Virginia Theological Seminary

Starting with childhood memories from Pine Lake in Bristol, Connecticut, to dramatic moments of intervention and reconciliation in Guayaquil, Ecuador, Bishop Howe has given us a remarkable tapestry that unfolds his personal story with cataclysmic theological struggles within the Church. His recounting of the 3 R's conference in Winter Park, Florida in 1986 highlights an intersection where three movements of renewal came together in common purpose and laid the structure for what was yet to come. His telling is warm and personable while also provocative as it delineates the steps that brought many leaders, including himself, to a reluctant acceptance of Anglican realignment. This book is and will remain a significant account of the history of the Anglican world for centuries to come. This is a very important work in my opinion and covers territory nobody else has addressed.

> The Very Rev. Dr. Henry L. Thompson III ("Laurie")
> Dean and President Emeritus, Trinity School for Ministry

I love testimonies, and John Howe's deeply personal book is full of accounts of God's gracious work of salvation and healing. Even those who know him well will be likely astonished by the extraordinary fruitfulness of his rich and varied ministry. His commitment to the Word of God and his embrace of the fullness of life in the Holy Spirit marked him as a leader of tremendous influence to generations of church leaders. Having served alongside him as a fellow rector in our diocese, I am keenly aware of the great influence he has had through Bible teaching and healing prayer, in leading his parish to 50% outreach, and by helping to establish such ministries as NOEL (now Anglicans for Life), CMJ-USA (a Christian Ministry to Jewish People), and Trinity School for Ministry—a life truly bearing "fruit that abides" (John 15:16).

> The Right Rev. John A.M. Guernsey
> First Bishop of the Diocese of the Mid-Atlantic, ACNA

I am astounded by John Howe's memoir! We have been friends for many years, and yet I never realized all that had been accomplished during his years at St. Stephen's, Truro and then at Lake of the Woods Church as classic examples of what Christ's Church can be. I honor John's full and faithful life as it is so well reflected in this book, but I also pray that it will be read by all those who are looking for ways in which Christian churches can fulfill the purpose for which God created them in the first place.

Harry C. Griffith
Founder, Bible Reading Fellowship (U.S.),
Former Executive Director, Anglican Fellowship of Prayer

There are simply some stories that need to be told. Bishop John Howe's story is one of those.

He skillfully takes us through elements of his life where Jesus was clearly present and guiding him. While I have read other books he has written, along with his spectacular wife, Karen, this is a book that fills in gaps. Having known Bp. John Howe for decades, nonetheless, this book contained new information and even surprises. I encourage you to accept his invitation to enter into his journey with Jesus, and I commend this book to you with a great sense of gratitude for his years of faithfulness.

The Rt. Rev. Keith L. Ackerman
Eighth Episcopal Bishop of the Diocese of Quincy

Bishop John Howe is truly a man sent from God. The Lord sent him into a turbulent period of upheaval in the Church's history, and his story reveals the precision of the Lord's timing as he led one of the great parishes in the Episcopal Church and then the Diocese of Central Florida through the very stormy seas of change. I commend his book to anyone looking for direction and faithfulness in a time of uncertainty.

Reid Carpenter
Founder, Leadership Foundations, Inc.

While The Episcopal Church considers itself both catholic and protestant, the evangelical wing of The Episcopal Church has never dominated the church; it has nonetheless been a vibrant force for renewal within its ranks. One such person who led the charge for renewal is Bishop John W. Howe, a noted charismatic evangelical whose life and ministry spanned nearly six generations in the church. In this memoir, John brings to life his own career path, from the early days of his conversion through various chaplaincy and parish ministries, bumping into people who would themselves prove to be leaders in the call for renewal. Despite the ups and downs (mostly downs) of the growing apostasy in the church, John never lost sight of his Lord, his calling and mission to proclaim Christ and Him crucified. As Bishop of Central Florida, he went head-to-head with many of the leaders of the Church, never losing sight of his faith, even as The Episcopal Church imploded over sexuality issues. Bishop John held his ground, finally conceding defeat by leaving the denomination and joining the Anglican Church in North America over the passage of a resolution mandating homosexual marriage. It was a bittersweet end for the evangelical bishop, but he left with his head held high, concerned more about honoring God than the dictates of a church that changed its teaching on marriage. I recommend this book to anyone thinking of ministry and the cost of discipleship.

David W. Virtue DD
VIRTUEONLINE

Foreword

When I was a senior in high school, I was invited to participate in a discipleship course with Young Life. We met each week for teaching, fellowship, prayer, and to discuss our assignments from the previous week. We would be assigned books and articles to read and a specific Scripture to memorize. One of our assigned readings was *Which Way? A Guide for New Christians* by John and Karen Howe. This little book was written to help new believers in their relationship with Jesus Christ.

Reading *Which Way? A Guide for New Christians* was my first exposure to John Howe. Years later, when I was an Episcopal priest, I began to listen to his sermons and teachings while he was a rector as they were very practical and helpful for one who was seeking to follow Jesus and walk in the power of the Holy Spirit. Later, as a bishop I was able to support Bishop John as he stood for the Christian Faith and the morality of the Bible. He was a great encouragement to me and so many others who were seeking to make sense of the Episcopal Church's departure from Biblical Christianity.

Be to the Flock a Shepherd is a refreshing tale of John Howe's life, walk of Faith, and ministry. But it is so much more! It is a series of teachings and lessons in how to walk with God, hear his voice, obey his command, and be empowered with the Spirit.

You will laugh, cry, ponder, and be challenged to walk with Jesus closer than you currently are. His example of following Jesus in his marriage, family life, and ministry is quite an inspiration.

Psalm 107:2 says: *Let the redeemed of the Lord say so*; and I Peter 3:15 says: *In your hearts regard Christ the Lord as holy, always being prepared to make a defense to anyone who asks you for a reason for the hope that is in you yet do it with gentleness and respect."* These verses are modeled in the life of John Howe and reflected in *Be to the Flock a Shepherd*.

The Lord be with you.

The Most Reverend Foley Beach
Archbishop and Primate of the Anglican Church in North America
(2014-2024)

Table of Contents

Chapter one – In the Beginning..1
Chapter two – I Have Decided to Follow Jesus..............................31
Chapter three – Preparing for Ministry..63
Chapter four – Mixed Responses...74
Chapter five – Call to Parish Ministry...95
Chapter six – Truro, A Local Ministry Reaching Out to the World..106
Chapter seven – Expand the Tent..150
Chapter eight – Come Up Higher..165
Chapter nine – A New Beginning at Lake of the Woods..............198
Chapter ten – Tying Up Some Loose Ends.......................................205

Appendix A: Louis Howe's Feldspar Mine.......................................208
Appendix B: Grandma Jessie Howe's Long Island Clam Chowder (Recipe)..209
Appendix C: A Brief History of Trinity School for Ministry..........210
Appendix D: The Stones Cry Out..212
Appendix E: Resolution of 69th General Convention of the Episcopal Church 1988..216

Amazon/Kindle
ISBN: 9798329182859

Bishop John W. Howe
bcf3@aol.com

Holt Publishing
HoltPublishing4U@gmail.com

Copyright 2024
All Rights Reserved

Cover Art Created by Claudia McKinney

BE TO THE FLOCK A SHEPHERD
Bishop John W. Howe

Chapter 1

In the Beginning

We are what he has made us, created in Christ Jesus for good works, which God prepared beforehand to be our way of life (Ephesians 2:10).

My farthest-back memories are of my grandparents, so let me start there. My grandfather on Dad's side, Louis Wadsworth Howe, was born in 1870 in what was then the small town of Glastonbury, Connecticut. Just five years had passed since the Civil War ended and Abraham Lincoln was assassinated. (Had Lincoln not died at age 56 it is conceivable that my grandfather might have known him!) Grandpa was 46 when my dad was born, 72 when I came into the world.

When Grandpa was a young man, cars didn't exist (the first real one was built in 1885). Nor did telephones (they began to be used in 1876), electric lights (introduced around 1880), movies (1887), radio (earliest use was in 1897), airplanes (the Wright brothers first flew in 1903), or television (commercially available since the late 1930s). The first reliable flush toilets in America were built (by Thomas Crapper) in the 1880s; before that there were outhouses and chamber pots. There were no computers, no Internet, no cell phones. What an amazingly different world it was!

My grandfather completed only two years of high school. To get to school he had to finish his chores on his father's farm, then ride a horse down to the Connecticut River, leave the horse in a pasture, row his boat across the river (about a mile at that point), climb the hill to catch a train in Wethersfield, and take it into Hartford, about 45 minutes away. Of course, he had to repeat the pattern in reverse at the end of the school day.

Grandpa worked the farm along with his father, but he wanted to go "out west" to be a sheep rancher. Instead, his dad said, "If you stay here, I will buy a general store, and we can run it together." He stayed. From very old photographs it reminds me of the Mercantile on the television program "Little House on the Prairie."

"J.W. Howe & Son" had the first telephone in Glastonbury, Connecticut. If someone wanted to call a friend - say in Boston - he would write ahead to make an appointment: "I will call you a week from Saturday. Please be at the local pharmacy [or wherever there was a corresponding telephone] at 10 AM to receive my call."

When Grandpa bought his first car there were four other automobiles in Glastonbury: a Packard, two Model A Fords and a "one-cylinder Cadillac that moved ahead by a series of short jumps" (Grandpa's description).

After several years at the general store Grandpa became a miner, digging some 70,000 tons of feldspar out of the hills of South Glastonbury.[1] He built a railroad line to carry the feldspar out of the mine. He bought large tracts of real estate, and became a landlord, and then he developed a water company to provide for his tenants.

---

[1] Feldspar is mined from granite, and it is used in making glass, ceramics, pottery, soaps, and abrasives for household cleansers. See Appendix A

He was for a brief time a state senator, and over his long life he built an impressive portfolio of blue-chip stock holdings.

In 1919, when a group of businessmen wanted to begin the Glastonbury Bank and Trust, they came to my grandfather and asked him to become its president. "I don't know anything about banking," he responded. "Yes, but you are an honest man," they insisted. He accepted their offer and remained president into his late seventies and chairman of the board until he died at age 98.

In 1930, during the Great Depression, "runs" on many banks across the nation caused them to fail as depositors rushed to withdraw their funds. Grandpa met personally with each of his depositors and convinced nearly all of them not to do that. Both their deposits and the bank itself were saved.

Grandpa was twelve years older than my grandmother, Jessie Mae Tyler, and he ran the Sunday school at St. Luke's Episcopal Church when she began attending. "Little girl, when you grow up, I'm going to marry you," he declared. And he did; he was 39, she was 27.

My dad was the third of their four children; the other three were all girls.[2] When all four of them were children they contracted scarlet fever, and the family physician told Grandpa to "Get them to some place that is cool and breezy."

Grandpa chose a section of Old Saybrook called Cornfield Point, on the Connecticut shoreline of Long Island Sound, near the mouth of the Connecticut River. He built two cottages, side by side, just across the street from the beach, and Dad's eldest sister later married the only son of the couple who owned the third cottage on that block. There were only five cottages on the whole point in those

---

[2]The birth order was Mary, Emma, Dad, and Ruth.

days; today there are thousands. Many of my fondest growing-up times were spent going from one cottage to the next, and joining whatever conversations, games, or other activities were happening at the time.

Grandpa sent all four of his children to college, in Dad's case Wesleyan University in Middletown, Connecticut, where he studied economics, and afterward he went to work for the Phoenix Insurance Company in Hartford (now part of Traveler's) where he eventually earned the nickname "Mr. Inland Marine" for the kind of insurance he majored in developing. After a couple of years there he met my mom, who worked at the Phoenix as a secretary and switchboard operator.

Mom was an only child. She and her parents, Glen and Agnes Roberts, lived on the edge of Pine Lake in Bristol, Connecticut, not far from the University of Connecticut, which I would attend many years later. "Gram" had gone through two difficult marriages before meeting Glen, whom my mother nicknamed "Poppy." He was a quiet, unassuming man who delighted in his adoptive family. Mom's biological father was Hilding Hanson (who I never met).

"Gram" and "Poppy" were decades younger than my father's parents, and they both worked for an automobile dealer in Hartford, about thirty miles from their home. Most of the year it was a pleasant enough drive, but in the winters it could be brutal.

Gram and Poppy's home was much smaller and less formal than that of my Howe grandparents. But an amazing warmth was there to greet us whenever we visited. Usually, Dad had two weeks' vacation in the summer, and we would typically spend a couple of days in Glastonbury, four or five more in Old Saybrook, and another week at the Lake in Bristol. Gram had a small bookcase in her living room that was just for my two younger sisters and me. It had three shelves, with one shelf reserved for each of us. When vacation rolled around each summer, we would arrive to find the bookcase stocked to overflowing with new toys and goodies.

Dad and Mom – John[3] and Shirley - were married just two months before the bombing of Pearl Harbor, and Dad's company transferred him from Connecticut to the Windy City of Chicago, (where I made my debut a little more than a year later). Dad couldn't join the army because of a back injury he had suffered as a teenager during a pickup basketball game. Jumping for a rebound he had fallen against the corner of a stone bench on the sideline, and he wore a brace for the rest of his life. Happily, most of the time he coped well.

My parents' first home was a one-bedroom apartment in downtown Chicago, a short drive from Dad's work. And on November 4, 1942, I arrived to join them.

For the first few months of their married life my father kept a meticulous notebook, recording - literally - the menu for every meal they shared, and the cost of every item they purchased. Here, for instance, is part of a grocery list from the first month after they were married, in October 1941:

2-pound jar raspberry jam	.29
2-pound jar peanut butter	.26
2 heads of lettuce	.15
2 cans of peas, 17 oz. each	.25
1 pound bacon	.42
1 pound pork chops	.39
1 pound sausage meat	.45
1 pound salt	.07

---

[3] Dad was originally "John II" named after his grandfather. He dropped the "II" when his grandfather died. I was originally "John Jr." I dropped the "Jr." when Dad died.

1 loaf bread	.07
TOTAL	$2.35

Mom was in the hospital for a full week when I was born. The bill for room, board, obstetrical fees, nursery, delivery, medicines, and lab work came to a total of $61.85. (So, I know *exactly* what I am worth!)

It is a strange thing to awaken to the sound of gunfire. And stranger still to have that as the very earliest of all my memories. But there it is, the farthest-back thing I can recall: the sound of rat-a-tat-tat on the radio, machine guns killing people on both sides of the terrible conflict we had entered during World War II. Of course, I didn't know what it was, or understand what it meant, until much later.

We lived in Chicago for my first three years, and I have only two other memories from those days. Mom used to take me to a park where swing sets stood in a sandy area near a pond - or perhaps it was a swimming pool. I know other mothers and children were there, as well, but I don't remember any interaction with them. But I do remember the swings: up and back, up and back I flew. I know my earliest days were happy ones.

And there were Garret and Margie. Margie was the horse that pulled Garret's milk truck. She knew her route so well that Garret could jump off while she kept plodding along: clip, clop, clip clop - as he ran up to each apartment stoop to deliver one- or two-quart bottles of fresh milk, each with a thick layer of cream on top, and pick up the empties to be washed and refilled at the dairy. Margie had a nose bag full of oats, so she could eat as she walked, and blinders on the sides of her eyes to keep her from being startled by anything unexpected.

When I was not quite a year old my parents brought me "home" to meet all four of my grandparents in Connecticut, and I was baptized in St. Luke's Episcopal Church, Glastonbury where Mom and Dad had been married two years before. My Dad's oldest sister and her husband were my godparents.[4]

Little did I know how much time I would come to spend in that church, and so many others, in the years to come!

My sister, Sherry, was born in 1945, and our little downtown apartment was far too small for our growing family. We moved about 15 miles west of Chicago to the small suburb of LaGrange Park. My parents bought a three-bedroom house with just one bathroom at the top of a long, hard flight of stairs. (I remember falling down them at least twice when I was still very young)

World War II was just ending, but Dad planted a "victory garden" in the vacant lot next door. The government had encouraged everyone who had enough land available to do that during the war years when many foods were being rationed. I remember thinking there was nothing that tasted quite as good as corn picked from the stalk, shucked, and boiled immediately. There was an apple tree in the backyard, and before long I learned to climb it. On occasion, Mom would let me take a sandwich with me, and I would eat lunch in that tree.

We had a coal burning furnace in the basement, with a window next to the driveway. In the fall a coal truck would arrive with the delivery for the coming cold months and pour about half a ton of coal down a chute into the storage room next to the furnace. When I was old enough to help, it became my job to shovel the coal directly into the furnace each evening before going to bed. Sometime around 1950 we got a "stoker" that made the job

---

[4]Mary and Paul Parshley.

somewhat easier. That was an electric machine that held several days' supply of fuel, and automatically delivered it into the furnace as it was needed. Still, I had to put the coal into the stoker, and going down into that dark basement at night was always scary! We would live in that house for the next nine years, and there I would have my first conscious awareness of God.

C.S. Lewis famously told of his conversion on top of a British double-decker bus. He reported getting on a skeptic and getting off a believer, becoming, "perhaps, that night, the most dejected and reluctant convert in all England." Lewis said, "I know very well when, but hardly how, the final step was taken…. When we set out, I did not believe that Jesus Christ is the Son of God, and when we reached the zoo, I did."[5]

In my life there was no such single event, but a whole series of moments in which the Lord pressed in upon me, and made me know his reality, his love, and - finally - his lordship.

Sherry and I had twin baby-sitters, Jean and Joan Dixon. The girls always shared their responsibility for us, and one day, when I was about 3 ½ years old, they asked my parents if they could take me to church (Sunday School) with them. "What kind of a church is it?" my father asked. "Episcopal," they replied. My folks thought that was safe! Dad had been raised an Episcopalian, and Mom a Roman Catholic. Although they were married in St. Luke's they had not yet gotten involved in any local congregation. "The Twins' Church," was Emmanuel Episcopal, a little more than a mile from our home, and the three of us could walk there in about 20 minutes.

Nearly eight decades later I can still recall the first time I went there. The lights were subdued, the air was cool, voices were hushed. I didn't know the word back then, but there was a sense of

---

[5]C.S. Lewis, *Surprised by Joy* (New York: Harcourt, Brace and Company, 1955), p. 224 ff.

holiness about the place. It was all unfamiliar, but somehow I knew I was home.

Mostly we went to "children's chapel," and only rarely attended the "big church." But there were songs and skits and coloring books, flannel graphs and crosses and candles. There were stories about Abraham and Sarah, an elderly couple who finally had the son God had promised them years before. God asked Abraham to sacrifice that very son but spared him at the last minute when Abraham proved he was willing to obey. The son's name was "Isaac," whose name meant "laughter," and the whole story was both bittersweet and funny at the same time.

Then there were stories about Isaac and his beautiful wife, Rebekah, and their son, Jacob, who tricked his brother Esau out of his "birthright;" and their grandson, Joseph and his "coat of many colors." We learned of Moses, who parted the Red Sea, Joshua, who "fit the battle of Jericho," Daniel, and David, and so many others, and of course…Jesus.

Out of all the great heroes Jesus was clearly Number One. He could change water into wine, heal sick people, cast out evil spirits (whatever *they* were), still violent storms, walk on water, raise people from the dead, find lost sheep, and drive money-changers out of the Temple. He died on a cross for our sins (that seemed to mean he was punished for what we did wrong), and then he rose from the dead himself! He wore a white robe, and he had long hair, and there was a glow around his head. And after he came alive again, he floated up into heaven to be with God. I didn't understand how all of that "worked," but I was fascinated by the stories.

And there was Miriam Beath, the Superintendent of Church School (a *very* impressive title to a three-year-old!); she always gave us a brief sermonette. I remember just one of her talks. "Children," she began, "on the way to church this morning the Lord Jesus told me to tell you..." I have *no idea* what she said next! I was arrested at the thought of *Jesus* speaking to *her*. You mean you *know* him...today? Amazing! How can you know someone who lived so long ago and so far away? How can you talk with someone who is in heaven with God while you are on your way to church? It was many years before I even began to have answers to such questions. But a "seed" was planted in my young life. I am forever grateful that Jean and Joan introduced me to church, and thankful for all that followed from that introduction.

When I was four, my mother gave birth to twins: my brothers William and James, whom she had carried for only seven months. Had it been today there is little question they would have made it with the medical technology now available, but in 1946 they survived only a few hours apiece. My parents' first thought was to simply have the hospital "take care of" their bodies. But then Dad said, "We can't do that. They lived a little while. We gave them names. Let's call that church John has been attending. Maybe the minister can help."

Fr. Everett Carr arrived almost immediately. He listened carefully and attempted to console my parents. He prayed for them, and then he said, "I'm scheduled to be out of town this weekend; I will ask my Assistant to do the funeral for you." He picked up the telephone...then put it down again. "No, this is more important." Whatever it was that had been scheduled he canceled for a grieving couple he had never previously met. And my parents saw Jesus reaching out to them through Fr. Carr that day. With his help they got through their loss.

For the rest of her life Mom almost never missed a Sunday in church. She always sat in the very front pew. (Dad didn't become a regular churchgoer until several years later. That's another story I will tell in a bit.) My twin babysitters brought me to church with them. The death of my twin brothers brought my mother there as well.

My father invested deeply in me when I was young. Together we joined the YMCA's Indian Guides. Dad was Big Chief Flying Cloud, and I was Little Chief Flying Cloud. A couple of years later, I became a Cub Scout. Most Cub packs had Den Mothers. My pack had a Den Father – mine. Later he encouraged my participation in the Boy Scouts as well. He helped me through many of my merit badges, including one for cooking. I made plank steaks for us and cooked them in aluminum foil in the coals of a wood fire. (They were pretty dreadful, but Dad ate his without comment.) But let me back up a bit.

Less than a year after the twins died, Mom was expecting again. I am pretty sure my parents hoped to fill the void that followed losing the two boys as soon as possible. We anticipated that the newest addition to the family (my sister Linda, as it turned out) would arrive in early August. But Dad had a two-week vacation, and he had to take it, or he would lose it. He decided to go back to Connecticut, and I would go with him: just the two of us guys. Mom didn't feel up to making the trip, so she and Sherry stayed home. Dad and I took the "little train," the daily commuter, from LaGrange to Chicago, and then got onto the "big train," with dining and sleeping cars, overnight from Chicago to Hartford.

In 1947 most of the nation's trains were still being pulled by steam engines. To a small boy there were few things as exhilarating as hearing the conductor call out "All Aboard." Far ahead the engineer would blow his horn - two long, mournful howls like those of a wolf at the moon – and the mighty "Iron Horse" would begin huffing and puffing as it started to roll: choo…choo…choo…choo…choo…choo…choo…choo…CHOO…CHOO – all the while belching a stream of smoke and ash. And as the train achieved its cruising speed the clackety-clack of wheels over the welded joints of the rails beneath became a kind of heartbeat suggesting that this "Horse" itself was very much a living thing.

It was only a couple of hours to our first stop in Elkhart, Indiana, where my cousins, Jim and Janet Waddington, lived. Uncle Les and Aunt Emma brought them to see us for a few minutes on the platform before the train was scheduled to resume the journey. They brought me a box of Animal Crackers to snack on. But, as we lingered a moment too long, the train began to move! Dad grabbed me by the hand, and we ran. The conductor saw us coming, and he left the retractable stairs in the "down" position. Dad grabbed me under my arms and handed me up to him before leaping onto the bottom stair himself. I don't think we were ever in danger of being left behind; the start-up for those big locomotives was much too slow. But, for a five-year-old, being handed to a conductor through the open door of a moving train was about as exciting as it gets!

Dad and I had a "roomette," a small private compartment with two benches that faced each other, and its own attached lavatory with a stainless-steel sink and commode. "Flushing" the toilet meant opening a small trap door that allowed waste to drop onto the track bed where – (theoretically, at least) it would decompose and wash away.

During the afternoon we played checkers and Dad read stories to me, and at one point we took the long walk through a dozen or more cars to the very back of the train, the "observation car" where lounge chairs and tables were available for any of the passengers to use and refreshments were served by a steward in his crisp white uniform (not that I needed any; I had my Animal Crackers!) Getting from one car to another meant opening a large door and stepping onto the first of two metal bridges (or platforms) butted against each other above the "knuckle coupling" between the cars, stepping very gingerly from one platform to the next, and finally opening a second door into the adjacent car. The cars themselves were air conditioned, but the "vestibules" between them were not. But often the windows above them were left open and the air rushing past the train was pungent with coal smoke.

Back in the observation car I liked sitting in a chair facing the large, rounded window at the rear of the car, where endless miles of track stretched back to where we had been a few moments before. Most of our journey was through the very flat Midwest, but the scenery changed from farm areas to woodlands and then to cities and towns, the train occasionally stopping to allow travelers to board or disembark. But soon enough the conductor came through announcing, "Dinner is served in the dining car." And Dad and I returned, first to our roomette to wash up, and then on to the second car of the train where individual tables, each seating up to four people, were set with crisp white linen tablecloths and napkins and all the utensils for dinner. I have no idea what we had to eat, but I do remember the fun of sitting together and watching so much countryside going by.

When we finished dinner, we went back once again to our roomette. But now we found it had been completely transformed! Instead of the two seats facing each other there was a full-sized bed with the blankets turned down ready for us to climb in. After we changed into pajamas Dad asked if I wanted to "say my prayers." Of course that meant: "Now I lay me down to sleep...." When I finished I asked if he would say his. He did. It was the first time I ever heard my dad pray, and it would be many years before I heard him do so again. But I noticed that his prayer was not at all like mine – something memorized which I repeated every night. Dad roamed all over the board in his prayer, though it seemed to be mostly about our family. I remember wondering how he could know what to pray if it wasn't something he could recite.

Before we dropped off to sleep Dad pulled up the shade for one more look out the window. The moon was shining brightly and just then the train was crossing a wide river on a long bridge that curved to the left. We could look far ahead to see the engine and coal car pulling us, and we could look all the way back to the observation car far behind. The whole train was visible from our window, and still farther ahead, reflected in the water, were the twinkling, dancing lights of the city on the other bank. It was an unforgettable moment of wonder and beauty. We pulled down the shade. "I'll see you in the morning, Daddy." "Yes, son, I'll see you in the morning."

Some twenty-eight years later when my dad was dying, I asked him if he remembered that train trip. "Of course." "Do you remember then we lifted the shade and saw the whole train stretched out before us, going over that river?" "Oh yes, I do remember."

"Well, Dad, you're about to cross another 'river,' and this time you're going to meet Jesus on the other side. Dad, I'm going to miss you. But I'll see you in the morning." By then he had come to know the Lord, and he knew where he was going. But once again I'm getting ahead of myself.

About two years after my twin brothers died one of my father's friends passed away as well. I had never met the man, and we had no personal connection to any of his family. Dad said he wanted me to go with him to the funeral. The church was about an hour away, so we settled in for the ride.

Dad was still driving the 1941 Chevy coupe convertible he had purchased just before he and Mom got married. It was black with red leather upholstery, and it had a knob on the steering wheel. I usually sat in the back seat, but today there were just the two of us, and I got to ride "up front." It was nice being together that morning – "just us guys" again.

My mother had not yet learned to drive, so that was totally "Daddy's car." He would leave every morning to drive a couple of miles to the train station where he would catch the commuter to Chicago. Then, in the afternoons he would return. Often, I would sit on the front stoop with my sister, Sherry, waiting to greet him. He would always drive home with his jacket on the back seat and his white shirt sleeves rolled half-way up his forearms.

That day on the way to the funeral we talked about many things, most of them having to do with school. I was a big boy now, in kindergarten, and I often walked the four blocks to school by myself. Sometimes I went with Tommy, who lived directly across the street. (No one questioned children walking to school by themselves back then.) Dad told me that many of the people coming to the service would be sad, and probably some of them would be crying. And he said his friend's body would be in a long box called a "casket." Some of the people would probably go up to look into the casket and say a prayer while they stood next to it, but we would not do that. We would just stay in our pew. I remember seeing the box from the front of the church and wondering what a body looked like. But I was glad I didn't have to find out just then. The service had some music and talking; the only part I recognized was The Lord's Prayer, which we had learned in Sunday School. A lot of the people talked with each other before and afterward. But we just slipped in and slipped out again.

I asked Dad what happens to people when they die. He said he thought they "went to be with God, in heaven, like Jesus." I said, "My Sunday School teacher said that Jesus went to heaven in his body, but your friend's body is still in the casket in church." Dad said he didn't understand it very well himself, but he thought that someday our bodies will go up to rejoin our souls, and we will live forever. But then he changed the subject. He said he wanted to tell me about another important thing: where babies come from. He said God made daddies' and mommies' bodies to fit together in a special way, and when that happened it sometimes was the beginning of a baby growing in the mommy's tummy. It was about the ickiest thing I had ever heard! But Dad said it wouldn't seem so when I got older. (He was right.)

He said this fitting together is a very wonderful way for a daddy and a mommy to show each other that they love one another, and when it does lead to a baby coming into their family it is even more wonderful. He said I would probably have questions about this as I was growing up, and he wanted me to know I could always ask him any of my questions. He said I would hear some words I wouldn't understand, and he would always be willing to explain them to me. I remember thinking this was the most "grown-up" talk we had ever had together and, even though it was about things I really didn't care very much about at the time, I realized it was "important."

Suddenly the passenger door I was leaning against on the ride home flew open and I found myself falling from the moving car. But Dad was able to grab my arm and pull me safely back inside. It happened so quickly I didn't have a chance to be scared. But I realized later it was almost a disaster. During a very carefully orchestrated introduction to the mystery of sex and the funeral of his friend, my father ended up saving me from what could have been my own demise, as well. I have always thought it remarkable that he introduced me to the "facts of life" and the "facts of death" on the same day. "A time to be born, and a time to die."

Gram and Poppy lived on the shore of Pine Lake, in Bristol, Connecticut. Today it is a state park. In the 1940s their small house, with knotty pine paneling, was on a large lot where tree needles were so thick they prevented any grass from growing. The lot sloped down to a narrow road, then continued sloping on the other side down to the edge of the lake. It was summer vacation, and this year we had come for a week with them to be followed by a week at "the shore" in Old Saybrook. My best present in Gram and Poppy's bookcase was a steel fishing rod and reel. Poppy said, "I'll show you how to use it tomorrow."

Next morning Poppy, Dad, and I headed for the lake. We all had rods, reels, and "fisherman's hats" (only mine was new). We had a can full of earthworms that Poppy dug up for our outing. He put a red and white bobber on my line, a hook on the end with a little lead weight just above it, and a worm on the hook. And he showed me how to throw the line into the water. He called it "casting," but in my case it was really just throwing. My line went in first, followed a moment later by Poppy's and Dad's. (They actually did cast, and their lines went a lot farther out into the lake than mine did.)

After only a few minutes there was a tug on my line, and my bobber disappeared beneath the surface! Poppy said, "Pull hard and quick!" I did. "Now reel him in." I turned the handle as fast as I could, and soon a small catfish came wriggling up out of the water. Poppy took him in a glove, and carefully extracted the hook from his mouth. "Still good to use again; you even have part of the worm left!" he said. And he dropped the fish into a bucket of water. "You got a bullhead," he exclaimed. I ran all the way back to the house to tell Gram and Mommy. It was even more exciting than being handed to the conductor on a moving train! "We will have it for dinner," Gram said. "See if you can catch some more."

I went back to the lake, and my line was already in the water. When Poppy handed me the rod it was clear there was another fish on the end. (Did he or Dad catch it while I was gone, and put it there for me? I never did find out.) I reeled it in, and this time it was a sunfish - "a pumpkinseed," Poppy said. Again, I ran up to the house to tell the news. And again, Gram said, "Go catch another." I went down to the lake a third time, and this time I did it *all by myself*. I baited the hook; I threw out the line. I gave a quick pull when I felt the tug. I reeled as quickly as I could. And I landed another catfish. Poppy still had to take it off the hook for me.

I caught "two bullheads and a pumpkinseed." And that night we had fish for dinner: mine, Dad's, and Poppy's. An amazing catch, indeed (but mine tasted best).

Summers were always the happiest times. Sometimes we went from "the shore" to "the lake," and sometimes it was the other way around. At Pine Lake the family consisted of just my parents, my sisters, and Gram and Poppy. But at the shore four families, plus Grandma and Grandpa Howe, filled three family cottages with a total of twenty-four relatives of all ages. At a family reunion a while ago, it was amazing to go around the room and hear from virtually every person what a special part Saybrook played in our growing-up-years.

Grandpa had originally planned to build just one cottage, with a separate garage. But putting up the first one took so long that he decided to turn the garage into a separate cottage, with garages in the basements of both buildings. Dad's eldest sister Mary had married Paul Parshley, whose family owned the third cottage on the block. Paul was an only son, who inherited the cottage from his parents. Eventually Paul and Mary had five children, four girls and a boy. So, theirs was "the Parshley cottage." Dad's youngest sister, Ruth, and her husband, Titus Hale ("Uncle Tite") and their four daughters, used the "Little Cottage" (originally planned to be the garage) in the middle.

And Grandma and Grandpa shared the "Big Cottage" with our family and Dad's sister Emma and her husband, Les, and their two children, Jim and Janet Waddington, who we had seen briefly at the train station in Indiana. They called it a "cottage," but it was an amazing house with five bedrooms on the second floor, two more on the third, and a large porch that could accommodate up to four more beds. The garage in the basement could easily hold two cars, though when I was older, I once squeezed three into it – just barely. It also had a workshop, three changing rooms, a shower for those heading to the beach across the street, and a coal burning stove for supplying the hot water throughout the house. Once again, it was my job to stoke the fire when we were there.

In those days folks would "stake out" their section of the beach by stretching out old blankets or quilts, sometimes with a large beach umbrella to provide some midday shade. The blankets and whatever "gear" people had could be left in place all day, even if they needed to go up to their homes for lunch or a bathroom break. At about two o'clock every afternoon the "Good Humor Man" would arrive with his truck filled with ice cream on sticks. My favorite (to this day) was vanilla with a toasted almond shell.

At night the Parshleys and the Hales would leave their rowboats upside down on the beach tied to hooks in the sea wall alongside the other two dozen boats similarly tied. Everyone knew the owners of each boat, and there was never any concern they would be stolen or damaged. There was also tubing. Grandpa kept half a dozen old inner tubes of varying sizes, each with several patches on it, in the basement. They made fine bucking broncos when the waves were strong. I discovered an old wooden ironing board that I tied atop two tubes to make a small raft.

Long wooden jetties stretched from above the high tide water line out into the surf to keep the shifting sands from drifting away altogether. The jetties were covered with thousands of snails and shiny, black-shelled mussels we would crack open and use as bait for fishing and crabbing. At low tide we would "walk the mud flats" – sand bars that emerged fifteen to twenty yards offshore and stretched along the beach as far as we could see.

No matter how hot the day, the firm wet sand beneath our feet was cool and refreshing. And, as we walked, every so often a small squirt of water between our toes would signal that a clam was burrowing just beneath the surface. Digging swiftly with a small hand rake or our bare fingers could produce a tasty morsel for dinner. A dozen clams would be enough for my grandmother's famous chowder. She had her own recipe using a clear broth. Grandma's "Long Island Clam Chowder" called for salt pork, onions, and potatoes, along with the clams, and she made it in a huge kettle that simmered for hours and lasted for days, getting better and better the longer it remained on the stove.[6] We took turns chopping the ingredients in a large wooden bowl with a special knife like the Ulu used by Alaskan and Canadian Eskimos. We enjoyed "Chowder parties down by the seashore every Fourth of July," as the old song put it.[7]

I remember one Fourth in particular. All the cousins from all four families were there, and other relatives kept arriving throughout the day. Grandpa had purchased an enormous supply of fireworks, and he divided it up between all of us, a large box apiece. There were sparklers and pin whirls, cherry bombs and worms, mortars, pasteboard tubes filled with combustibles, stars, and rockets. Setting off one after another after another took at least two hours - and (amazingly) nobody got hurt! It was a great day, with the flashing staccato and acrid scent of thousands of mini bombs filling the air that afternoon on the beach. I wondered whether life could ever be as fun as that annual holiday at Cornfield Point.

Back at home, my friend Dick was a year older than I. Somehow, at age 9 he got the job of delivering about five hundred advertising brochures on a Saturday. He asked me to help and said he would share the money he was being paid, a penny apiece – a whopping five dollars: a small fortune for two youngsters in 1950. He had a red Radio Flyer wagon, and we loaded it up. "Shouldn't take long," he said confidently. But after the first hour we had only distributed about 100 brochures. And we gave out another hundred or so during the second hour. As noon approached, we were hot, thirsty, and tired. And we had distributed less than half of the papers.

---

[6]See Appendix B for Grandma's recipe.
[7]*Dearie*, David Mann and Bob Hilliard, 1950

Dick said, "Why don't we just ditch them? Who will ever know?" I knew that wasn't right, but, after all, it was *his* job, not *mine*. So, I agreed. There was a large overgrown field nearby, with a natural hollow in the middle of it, a perfect dumping place. Over went the wagon, and we made our way home.

"Back so soon?" asked Dad. "Yes. It didn't take as long as I thought it would." "Are you sure you delivered *all* of them?" he inquired. I never figured out how he could always tell when I was not being truthful. But he could. And I told him the truth. "You are going to have to finish the job," he said. "But it's *Dick's* job," I retorted. "Dick is not my son; you are. You said you would help him, and he paid you for it. I want you to show me where the papers are. I'll drive you there." So, I took Dad to the field, and to the pile of papers lying just as we had left them. And he said, "I'll help you finish; let's do this together."

And we did. We put the papers in the trunk of the car, and Dad drove it about a half block at a time. Then he would stop, and he would do one side of the street and I the other. It took another two hours, but we did it all.

Last I heard Dick is in prison somewhere. (I'm not.)

When I was twelve, the Phoenix Insurance Company asked Dad to return to the "home office" in Hartford, Connecticut. The invitation seemed to imply that Dad would at some point become one of their officers, and it was expected that we would live in East Hartford, where nearly all the executives had their homes. But Dad was adamant that we should live in Glastonbury, his boyhood hometown, and he found a house on Boulder Circle, about three miles from where my grandparents lived. It was called "Boulder Circle" because where the Circle begins there is a fence and two huge granite boulders – more about that later. Neighbors said these massive stones were carried to that spot by glaciers during one of the ice ages.

In their later years my parents came to believe that the decision not to live in East Hartford might have cost Dad the officer position, but Glastonbury was a great place to spend my teenage years. I had several good friends during those special days "twixt twelve and twenty," but the one that stands out most is Dale. Somehow we bonded and found we shared interests as we navigated junior and senior high school.

We rode our bicycles all over town. One summer afternoon we happened upon a deep pool of water surrounded by steep granite walls, hidden in a wooded area. It was one of the most beautiful spots I had ever seen, and, of course, we took a swim in it. Later I learned we had "discovered" the feldspar mine my grandfather had shut down nearly thirty years earlier. It had long since filled with water in the intervening years.

Dale and I both made "go-carts" built on ancient power lawn mowers we purchased for about $25 apiece. (It took quite a while to save enough money to do that!) We found steering wheels in a junk yard, and front wheels from baby carriages, and by exchanging the flywheels that came with the mowers for much larger ones, we could make the carts go up to about eight miles an hour. (They were completely illegal for use on the streets, but no one ever stopped us.)

Dale lived about a mile from my house, and another mile beyond his house lay Roaring Brook, a fast-flowing tributary that twisted its way down the hills of Glastonbury to eventually join the Connecticut River. There were several good swimming holes along the Brook, but the best one was adjacent to Brainard Pond, a small man-made lake behind a dam, which was occasionally drained by opening the sluice gates at the back. We never swam in the Pond itself, but we discovered a natural swimming hole just downstream that we could get to by walking across the dam, where the water was never more than an inch or two deep, then dropping to some large, nearly flat rocks, and from there to a ledge where the water was knee-deep, and then to a wonderful hollow about the size of an Olympic swimming pool. There were always fish sharing the Brook with us, and occasionally we snagged one or two of them with handmade spear guns and cooked them over a fire on the shoreline. A couple of times Dale and I camped overnight next to the Brook and enjoyed fresh fish for breakfast.

I discovered I could crawl out my bedroom window onto the roof of the garage (we had no screens), drop down onto our garbage pails on the back side, and run down Sunset Drive to Dale's house on Hopewell Road. Then we would continue together through the woods and across the dam for a midnight swim. If our parents ever figured out we were doing that, they never mentioned it. Dale and I kept in touch over the years until I suddenly stopped hearing from him, and I realized he had gone to be with the Lord. I'm looking forward to the day we will perhaps swim together again in that great River that flows from the Throne of God.

It has been my great privilege to serve as pastor/rector of several truly wonderful churches, and for 23 years as the Bishop of the Episcopal Diocese of Central Florida, but it would be hard to think of much more modest beginnings at the start of my employment history. My earliest paid employment was for Grandpa Howe, starting when I was about 12, hoeing weeds from his large vegetable garden, and later reading the newspaper for him as his eyesight began to fail. He gave me one dollar per hour, and he was slightly grumpy about having to pay such exorbitant wages, but my father insisted it was the "going rate."

Dad's uncle, Louis Gilbert, lived on Main Street, almost at the foot of Chestnut Hill Road. The house he lived in had been one of the "stations" of the Underground Railway where runaway slaves were whisked down to the Connecticut River as they sought freedom. Uncle Lou always called my father "Jack," and Dad called him "Bill." (I never learned why Dad called him "Bill," but I began doing so, as well.) Occasionally, Bill would ask me to do odd jobs around his property. I would ride my bike the three miles downhill from Boulder Circle, and at the end of the day I would have to ride it those same three miles back again – this time *uphill*. One day, as I finished my chores for him, Bill asked if I would like a ride home. "Of course! Thank you!" We loaded my bike into the trunk of his car. "Would you like to drive?" I was fourteen; I could hardly believe it! "Yes, I would!" I had never tried to drive before, but I had watched carefully, and I had no trouble putting the car into gear, or even handling the clutch and "H" pattern of shifting. But when we got to the final turn onto Boulder Circle from Sunset Drive, I slowed the car. Half-way into the right turn I realized we were still going too fast, and I tried to hit the brake…but instead my foot hit the gas pedal!

We barreled through a split-rail fence and stopped beside the larger of the two boulders that gave the Circle its name. Neither of us was hurt, but the car was badly damaged. The police showed up within minutes and took Bill's story. But they didn't arrest either of us. (It was a very different time in America!) That incident became one of my favorite sermon illustrations.

Bill forgave me. That meant he didn't insist that I pay for the damage I had caused. (Not that I could have.) Instead, *he paid for it himself*: both his car and the neighbor's fence. That's how forgiveness works. When a person does something hurtful to someone else, the second person has two choices. He can either seek retaliation – he can try to make the offender pay for what he has done – or he can forgive the hurt. But, forgiving it doesn't make it go away. The person who forgives actually *pays for the hurt himself*.

When I was in college, I ruined a friend's sports jacket. And he forgave me. Which meant *he had to pay for it*. (You might want to be cautious about lending me things.) If you and I have offended against God – by our sin, our selfishness, by disregarding his instructions, by trying to "cross him out" of our lives – he has two choices, as well. He can insist we pay for what we have done, or he can "*pay for it*" himself. That's what God has done throughout all of human history. He has forgiven sinners. When he became one of us – in Jesus –we rejected him completely. We literally "crossed him out." He forgave even that. He didn't make us pay for it. He paid for it himself.

There was a strange epilogue to the car accident. About three weeks later an announcement came over the loudspeaker in my classroom: "Will John Howe please come to the Principal's Office." When I got there, Lt. Morgan, of the Glastonbury Police Department was waiting to see me. "You're John Howe?" "Yes, sir." "You smashed up your uncle's car and your neighbor's fence last month?" "Yes, sir. But my uncle was with me, and I had his permission to drive." "But you had no training, or a license to do so?" "No, sir." "You're pretty much of a bad boy, aren't you?" "No, sir. I don't think so." "You like smashing up cars, don't you?" "No, that was an accident, sir. I didn't like it, at all." "This isn't about your uncle's car; this is about your neighbor's car in the woods behind you."

I had no idea what he was talking about. Immediately behind our property Winston Smith had a very deep lot that ended in a wooded patch. And beyond that was a farm where several ancient cars and tractors had been abandoned and were slowly dissolving into rust. They had cracked and broken windows and ripped seats. I didn't know whether they had been vandalized or simply left to fall apart. I said, "I had nothing to do with any of that."

Lt. Morgan was not buying it. "I think you went out and deliberately smashed up your neighbor's car," he said. I insisted I had not. Over the next several minutes his accusations became stronger and stronger, and finally I realized he wasn't talking about the abandoned vehicles at the farm. Evidently, Win Smith had purchased a car for auto parts, and he kept it back in the woods behind his house. I knew nothing about it, but apparently, someone had attacked it. And since I was known to have smashed up my uncle's car – voila! I must have done it! "Where were you on April 14?" he asked. I couldn't remember.

There were no other adults present as this interrogation continued. I had no one to defend me. My parents didn't know this was happening. Finally, I said, "I'm telling you the truth. I had nothing to do with this. And I'm not going to answer any more questions." He let me return to class. I tried to make sense of what had happened. I was not a bad kid. I shouldn't have driven Bill's car, but he invited me to do so. What fourteen-year-old boy would have said No? And I had *not* done anything to Win Smith's car. I didn't even know it was there.

And suddenly I remembered. My friend, Hal Hunt, and his parents visited us all afternoon and evening on April 14. I asked the School Principal to call Lt. Morgan. "Are you ready to confess?" he asked. "No, sir. I can prove I didn't do it." And I did. It was the scariest time of my growing-up years. But being falsely accused was intriguing because I knew I was innocent. And that was great protection. I've been falsely accused of other things from time to time as a Christian leader. Having had that experience has stood me in good stead. Jesus warned that his followers will be falsely accused and dragged before the authorities. He said, "Do not worry about how you are to defend yourselves or what you are to say; for the Holy Spirit will teach you at that very hour what you ought to say." (Luke 12:11-12)

When I was 14, another uncle, Tite Hale,[8] got me a summertime job picking tobacco for the Consolidated Cigar Company, maker of Dutch Masters. Six days a week I would ride my bicycle about three miles down the hill from Boulder Circle to Main Street, where I would leave it at Bill Gilbert's house. Then I would be picked-up by a bus carrying workers – mostly from Jamacia – to the fields, about five miles away.

Connecticut shade tobacco is grown under "tents" (actually huge box-like nettings of cheesecloth which filters the sun, making for thinner, finer, more pliable leaves and offering some protection from insects). Tobacco is one of the fastest growing plants in the world. Seedlings a few inches tall are planted in straight lines beneath wires stretched from pole to pole in May, and by the Fourth of July they will have grown to nine feet in height. By the end of August, they may be over twelve feet high. In early June, my job, along with about thirty other teen-age boys, was to attach a length of string from the overhead wire to each of the plants below it. Over the next three months the plant would follow the string as it grew toward the top of the "tent."

There were five fields in all, and by the time we finished stringing the last one we were ready to return to the first field for "suckering" – removing the bottom three leaves of each plant to force the nutrients into the upper leaves. Each of the boys doing the suckering would pick the plants in two adjacent rows, alternating from left to right, left to right, and dragging himself on his bottom in the dirt between the rows. These first three leaves were too small to save, and they were simply discarded. There would be several additional pickings in which the leaves were taken to barns for drying. The soil was usually wet at this time of year, so by the end of our shift we were covered with mud and juice from the leaves. (And of course, I then had to take the bus back to where I had left my

---

[8]Married to my father's youngest sister, Ruth.

bike, and ride back *up* the three miles to home.) By the end of our day, we were as dirty and smelly as if we had been working in a pigsty.

When the suckering was finished, we were ready for the first of five pickings. The procedure was the same: we snapped the next three bottom leaves from each plant, but this time we kept them. We made "pads" of leaves from about four plants at a time, then left the pads on one side of the row or the other. When we finished the row, we got what resembled large laundry baskets, and pulled them between two rows, picking up the pads and stacking them, six pads on each layer, until the basket was full. Then, we repeated the process, row after row, pad after pad, basket after basket. We were paid by how many "bints" we picked, a bint being the portion of the row between two poles supporting the tent, about fifteen feet. Seven cents per bint. The fastest pickers among us could make what seemed a lot of money, $900 to $1,000 from June 1 to September 1. Adjusted for inflation, that would be about ten times that amount today.

Only boys, teenage and older, were in the fields back then, but girls and young women worked for the company as well, "sewing" the leaves together and hanging them from thin strips of wood, called laths, for drying in the barns. Most of the Jamaicans spoke some English, but they were more comfortable using "Jamaican Creole" or "Patwa" – a melodic combination of African languages and dialects that were brought to the island during the slave trade. The Jamaicans kept pretty much to themselves, as did the African Americans who came to Connecticut for the summer from Georgia and South Carolina. I was one of only a few "white boys." It was hard, dirty work, but I was proud to be making my own money, and I used my first paycheck to buy dinner for my family.

Two years later I was able to get a very different summer job, working at Midway Garage, pumping gas, and beginning to learn how to service automobiles. As the name suggested, Midway was located between two hills on Main Street - and I still had to ride my bike down in the morning and back up again in the late afternoon.

Gasoline cost twenty-four cents a gallon back then, and when a car pulled in, the attendant was expected to pump the gas *and* wash all the windows, check the air in the tires, the oil in the crank case, and the water in the radiator.[9] I had been on that job for about a month when a sudden thunderstorm popped up. Customer cars were parked on both sides of the street, and my boss, Jim Kristoff, said, "Go close the windows in all the cars." (This was long before air conditioning was standard in most automobiles, and most of the cars' windows were open.) I closed the windows on the Garage side of the street, and started to dash across to do the others, when a car coming around the bend and down the hill was traveling much too fast in the heavy downpour. In a split second I realized it couldn't stop in time to avoid hitting me.

I had just gotten my own driver's license about six months earlier, and the thought flashed through my mind: *I wonder how he feels, knowing he is about to hit me!* I have no recollection of what happened next. He did hit me, but somehow I stood up as Jim came running to help. "What happened?" I asked him, before collapsing into his arms. I woke up in the ambulance on the way to Hartford Hospital, and said,: "Call my mother," and gave them the phone number before passing out again. I woke up again in the Emergency Room, hearing a strange scraping sound. I asked the doctor, "Are you shaving my head?" He was. A gash on the back of it required forty-two stitches. My right eyelid was nearly torn off, and my right

---

[9]It was very like what Marty McFly witnessed at the Texaco station in Hill Valley in 1955 in *Back to the Future*, except there weren't four attendants; I had to do it all myself.

elbow was broken. Both legs were severely bruised. They said I would be in bed for at least a week, and in the hospital for a month.

Instead, I was out in four days. But that was the end of my career as an auto mechanic! My right arm was in a cast that bent at a thirty-degree angle, and when I went to Saybrook that summer I discovered I could swim on my left side, keeping my right arm out of the water like a periscope. And yes, it looked as weird as you imagine.

Three months later I asked Jesus to become my Lord, and many years down the road I came to realize there was a connection between surviving the accident and putting my trust in Christ. Like so many others who have gone through life-threatening experiences, I realized I had been miraculously spared by God, and if so, he had a claim on my life.

I was spared for God's purposes, and soon I would begin to discover what they were.

Chapter 2

I Have Decided to Follow Jesus

They explained the Way of God to him more accurately (Acts 18:26).

Tom was the captain of our high school basketball team, and a good friend. He asked if I would like to join him one Friday evening at "The Bible Club." "What is that?" I asked. "A couple dozen of us get together each week. We sing, play some games, and then learn about the Bible from Mrs. Wood. She's the wife of the Baptist minister." "Maybe some time," I said. "Not this week." The truth was I wasn't really interested at all. I respected the Bible, but I didn't think I needed to learn any more about it. After all, I had been going to Sunday School since I was three. But Tom kept asking me, nearly every week, for over a year. Somehow, I never did find the time.

But, in the middle of my junior year, I asked a classmate named Linda if she would like to go to a movie with me. "I'll have to pray about it," she said. I'll let you know on Monday." *Pray about it*! I had never heard an answer like *that* before! When Monday rolled around, I was eager to ask: "Well, did you get an answer?" "Yes. He said I can go out with you. But, instead of a movie, I wonder if you might like to go to The Bible Club next Friday. It meets in a different home each week." "Sure, I guess I can. Tom has been asking me about that for quite some time."

The first time I attended I was amazed to discover that nearly all of the most popular kids in our high school were there: our class president, the captain of the track team, the captain of the cheerleaders, members of the honor society, some of the lead singers from the Glee Club, various others, and of course Tom was there. He said he was glad I finally showed up. I was intrigued to discover that many of my classmates had been involved in the Bible Club for years. I wondered if there was a connection between being part of the Club and becoming the kind of person other kids wanted to be around. We played some silly games and had refreshments. Then the singing began. They sang several songs I had never heard before.

> "I'm satisfied with just a cottage below,
> a little silver and a little gold..."[10]

> "I may never march in the infantry, ride in the cavalry,
> shoot the artillery, and I may never zoom o'er the enemy,
> but I'm in the Lord's army..."[11]

> "I come to the Garden alone,
> while the dew is still on the roses..."[12]

> "Living for Jesus a life that is true;
> striving to please him in all that I do..."[13]

They seemed strange songs to me! Most of them talked about knowing God, knowing Jesus, like a best friend. Suddenly I remembered Miriam Beath from those early days of Sunday School: "Boys and girls, on the way to church this morning, Jesus told me to tell you..." She seemed to know him like a best friend; I hadn't encountered that again since I was three. But here, some of the most popular kids in my high school were talking and singing about knowing Jesus in almost embarrassingly personal terms. What was this all about? When the singing stopped, I began to find out as Mrs. Wood taught the scriptures. Actually, she simply told us stories from the Bible. But somehow, she made them so real, so contemporary and relevant that it was as if we were there.

---

[10] Mansion Over the Hilltop, Ira Stamphill (1949)
[11] I am in the Lord's Army, The New National Baptist Hymnal
[12] In the Garden, C. Austin Miles (1912)
[13] Living for Jesus, Thomas Chisholm, (1917)

I noticed she wore no make-up, and her only jewelry was her wedding ring. She was not beautiful in the way I had come to think of women being beautiful, but there was something attractive about her that drew and held our attention. I know now that what we saw was the Spirit of Jesus in her, and it was irresistible. I had seen it in Miriam Beath when I first went to Sunday School. Now I was seeing it in Ruth Wood; both of them had something about them that drew others – myself very much included – to them.

Jesus said, "When I am lifted up, I will draw all people to myself." (John 12:32) He was ultimately speaking about being "lifted up" on the cross, but we "lift him up" in our daily lives when we praise him, thank him, obey him, and share him with others. And whenever we lift him up, he draws people to himself. Mrs. Wood lifted Jesus up in the Bible Club, and he drew students from my high school to himself. And he began drawing me. The Bible Club quickly became part of my weekly routine. (Ironically, I never did go out with Linda!)

Mrs. Wood usually taught for about half an hour, and I was transfixed. I wanted her to never stop! But I also wondered: were there any *men* who knew God in this personal way? I was about to find out. One Friday night Mrs. Wood was sick, so her husband, Howard Wood, Pastor of the Pilgrim Baptist Church, substituted for her. He told the story of the prophet Elijah challenging the false prophets of Baal to a contest.[14]

Elijah said, "Let us prepare sacrifices. You prepare one for Baal, and I will prepare one for the Lord God of Israel. Then, let us call on our gods to consume the sacrifices by fire. The god who answers by fire is the true God." And all the people said, "That is a great challenge! Let's see who wins!" Elijah told the prophets of Baal to go first. From morning until mid-day, they called upon their

---

[14]From 1 Kings 18

god to answer them – but there was silence. Elijah mocked them: "Maybe your 'god' has gone on a journey, or maybe he's fallen asleep and must be awakened. Why don't you shout louder?" They did so; they shouted and danced and cut themselves with knives – all to no avail.

Finally, Elijah said, "Now it's my turn." He built an altar of twelve stones, put the wood in order, cut the sacrifice in pieces, and drenched it with twelve barrels of water. Then he called upon his God: "O Lord, God of Abraham, Isaac, and Israel, let it be known this day that you are God in Israel, and that I have done all these things at your bidding." And fire fell from heaven and consumed the sacrifice, the wood, even the stones, and all the water he'd poured. And the people declared, "The Lord, he is God; the Lord, he is God." One man faced down 850 false prophets, and he was entirely vindicated by the God who answered by fire! Howard Wood told his story as vividly as his wife told hers. Howard Wood knew the God of Elijah, and I wanted to know him too. I wanted to know him like Ruth Wood knew him, like the kids in the Bible Club knew him, like Miriam Beath knew him.

The Woods had a rustic cabin on a lake in New Hampshire, and on the last weekend of October 1959, they invited the whole Bible Club to go there on a retreat with them. We used sleeping-bags on the floor – boys in one part of the house, girls in another – and we waited in line to use the extremely pungent outhouse adjacent to the cabin. On Sunday, before we left for home, there was a time for sharing "testimonies": what has Jesus done in your life this weekend? I was arrested by what one of the guys told us. Harrison Moore (nicknamed "Dinty," after the beef stew), was captain of the track team, and an extremely popular student in our school. My impression, up to that point, was that Dinty was one of the most committed guys in the Club. But that afternoon he said he had only been going through the motions, and his relationship with Jesus was entirely superficial. "But," he said, "I have asked him to be my Savior this weekend, and I'm beginning a whole new life with him."

I was shocked. If *Dinty* was just going through the motions, what was *I* doing? If Dinty had to take a step beyond the superficial, what about me? When I got home from school the next day, I knelt beside my bed and said something like this:

"Lord Jesus, if you are really the way Pastor and Mrs. Wood say you are, if you really can be known the way my friends in the Bible Club say you can, if you can come into my life the way Dinty says you came into his…I want you to do that. I want you to be my Savior. I want to know you. And this is the day. Either it's all true, and you can do this in my life, or it is a horrible mind-game. If you make yourself known to me, I will follow you to the best of my ability for the rest of my life. But, if nothing happens before Mom calls me for dinner, I'm done with it. I'm not going to go back to the Bible Club or bother with church even one more time."

I now realize how presumptuous it was to pray that way, to demand that God meet me on *my* timetable. But Jesus promised, "Anyone willing to do the will of God will know the truth of my teaching." (John 7:17) I *wanted* to do God's will, if only I could know him! I don't know how long I stayed on my knees. It seems like it was the better part of an hour, but suddenly I had the overwhelming sense that I was in the very presence of God, and I *heard* him saying – not with my ears, but in my spirit – "You are saved." That's the way Baptists talk, and by now I had become used to it. Becoming a Christian, becoming a follower of Jesus, is a matter of being "saved" – and for many it is a once-in-a-lifetime datable moment. (Before it I was "lost;" now I am "found.") Episcopalians, and lots of others, usually put it differently. You will often hear someone from the more catholic wing of the Church say,

"I was saved, I am being saved, and I will be saved." There are good Biblical precedents for putting it both ways.

When St. Paul reported his life-changing encounter with the risen Christ to King Agrippa, he spoke of it as a moment – "at midday along the road" (Acts 26:13), – but when he wrote about it to the Philippians, he said it was still the goal of his life "to gain Christ and be found in him." (3:8-9) What happened to me on November 2, 1959, just before dinner, was both a life-changing moment *and* one stitch in a tapestry God has been weaving in my life from before I was born and would continue to weave for the rest of my life.

Within a year I faltered badly – I will tell of that momentarily – but over six decades later, I know it was real. Day by day I have gotten to know him better. There have been moments of rebellion and moments of doubt, but this living Lord Jesus has proven himself over and over again. "And he walks with me, and he talks with me, and he tells me I am his own. And the joy we share as we tarry there, none other has ever known."[15]

A few months later, one of Billy Graham's associates, named Jimmy Johnson, came to Hartford for a week of evangelistic meetings. Each night there was special music, congregational singing, and testimonies from well-known athletes and other celebrities. This led up to Johnson's strong Gospel presentation, followed by an "altar call" – an invitation to come to the front of the auditorium and "give your life to Jesus." Billy Graham was rapidly becoming one of the most admired men in the country, and his New York Crusade three years earlier had drawn unprecedented national attention.[16] Others were, like Jimmy Johnson, were holding similar

---

[15]In the Garden, Ibid.

[16]The 1957 New York Crusade began in Madison Square Garden on May 15 and was originally scheduled for five weeks. Because of its popularity it was extended twice – first to July 20, and then to September 1, for a total of 16 weeks. After the first extension, on what was planned to be the final night, July 20, over 100,000

meetings which usually drew warm and receptive audiences as well. America was experiencing what some people called a third "Great Awakening."

I attended three of Johnson's meetings, and I was thrilled when scores of people responded to the invitation by moving forward and praying the "sinner's prayer." Hearing the Gospel presented repeatedly in its most simple, straight-forward manner was very reassuring. Being a Christian involves both knowing *about* Jesus, and *knowing* him as a friend, companion, comforter, guide, protector, etc. Ultimately, these two dimensions must merge. The more we know *about* Jesus, the more we will be able to trust him day by day. And the more we trust him, and find him trustworthy, the more we will come to understand the things he said and did during his earthly ministry. The writer to the Hebrews said, "Jesus Christ is the same yesterday and today and forever." (13:8) So, we can expect there will be a coming together of our experience of Jesus in our personal lives and what we read of him in the scriptures. And that's why we love to hear the Gospel message again and again: "God loves you so much that he sent his Son, Jesus, to die on a cross that you might be forgiven. Receive him as Savior and Lord and be born again into eternal life both now and forever. And if you were the only one who needed him, God would have sent his Son to die for you."

Jimmy Johnson preached the Gospel with power and winsomeness, and I was deeply pleased to see so many stepping forward to receive new life in Christ. But on the final night of his meetings, Johnson's message was different. Instead of urging his

---

people jammed into Yankee Stadium, with another 20,000 outside, unable to get in. At the time, it was the largest crowd in the stadium's history. Ultimately nearly 2.4 million people attended the Crusade in person, and it was estimated that more than 100 million watched on television. 61,000 people were reported to have made "decisions for Christ" in the meetings.

listeners to "give their lives to Jesus" in a first-time commitment, he talked about *following Jesus* into "full-time ministry," and serving him as a pastor, a missionary, an evangelist, or in some other dedicated way. This time when he gave the "invitation" it was to *enlist for service*, and I went forward.

God used Jimmy Johnson to call me into ministry that night. I had no idea what it would entail, but I heard him as clearly as Simon and Andrew and James and John heard the call of Jesus as he "passed along the Sea of Galilee." "Follow me," he said, "and I will make you fish for people." "And immediately they left their nets and followed him." (Mark 1:16-18) And I did so that night.

How I wish I could say I never faltered, never wavered, in my commitment to Jesus. But I hit a huge roadblock the following year when I went off to college. I applied to several schools, but the one I was most interested in was the University of Connecticut, in Storrs – about 30 miles east of Glastonbury. My cousin, Jim, a year older than I, had enrolled there, and he invited me for a weekend early in his freshman year. I was very attracted to the place and thrilled when I received my acceptance a few months later.

Mrs. Wood told me there was a vibrant Chapter of the Inter-Varsity Christian Fellowship at UConn, headed by a student named Cal Fox. She said he was a leader beyond his years, and I would find a wonderful spiritual home in IVCF. She was right, but it was much more complicated than I anticipated. Cal had graduated by the time I got there, but he often returned to share with the UConn Chapter of IVCF.

I headed off to college looking for two very different kinds of students: committed Christians like those I had known in the Bible Club, and those as opposite to them as I could find – doubters, atheists, "freethinkers." I wanted to share my faith with them and, if possible, persuade them, just as St. Paul had done in so many of the places he visited on his missionary journeys. I wanted to learn how to argue theologically. And I wanted to hear the case for the opposition, learn its strengths and weaknesses, and attempt to answer its hard questions.

I found what I was looking for.

The Inter-Varsity chapter was small but strong. It held weekly meetings, often with guest speakers, in a comfortable lounge room at the Storrs Congregational Church. And there were nightly prayer meetings for the guys on the sixth floor of one of the men's dormitories. I began attending both meetings from the first week I hit campus. I tried going up and down the corridors of my dormitory inviting guys to a Bible Study in my dorm room. (A few showed up; one fellow came several times, and once a group gathered outside the door to loudly ridicule what we were doing.) I made a large poster of a quotation by D.L Moody and hung it above my desk:

"The world has yet to see what God can do with one man fully dedicated to him, And, with God's help, I hope to be that man."

I meant that and I tried to live into it. I began to be known as a Christian on campus, and when elections were held, I became the secretary/treasurer of the Inter-Varsity chapter, and I began rooming with Ken Lutters, the new chapter president. Inter-Varsity's strategy was to evangelize the secular university from within, student to student, professor to professor. IVCF staff members saw themselves as "coaches," with the faculty and students being the "players." We loved being coached by IV staff members: Peter Haile, Stan Rock, Linda Doll, and Bob Hill, who all encouraged us to be bold witnesses for Christ.

It was my job to correspond with our speakers, and we found there were some wonderful pastors in the area – and as far away as New Haven and Boston – who were willing to drive to Storrs to speak to our small group of collegians without reimbursement. We would cover their gasoline expense (and by then, it cost 27 cents a gallon) but we had no resources to do more than that. Those terrific men sensed a call from God to invest in the next generation, and they offered their wisdom and insights to us as a gift from the Lord.

Two of them were our favorites, and we invited them back repeatedly. Dr. Donald S. Ewing was the long-time pastor of the Trinitarian Congregational Church in Wayland, Massachusetts. He painted unforgettable word-pictures to illustrate the gospel:

> "If the sheep are lost, the shepherd must go where they are in order to rescue them. If they have wandered off into the darkness, he must plunge into that darkness to find them. If they have gotten caught in the brambles, the thorns that hold *them* are going to scratch and pierce *him*."

The other was Avi Brickner, a wonderful "Hebrew Christian." He was raised as an orthodox Jew, but he discovered Christ as a teenager, and he eventually persuaded his entire family to trust Jesus as their Messiah. Ordained as a Baptist pastor, Avi headed up a small outreach to Jewish people in the Boston area in a ministry called Israel's Remnant. Our chapter had him visit frequently, and he taught us many things about the Jewish background of the Christian Faith and about sharing our faith with Jews.[17]

These fine men, along with many others, helped us build on the faith foundations we brought with us to college. As St. Paul put it in his first letter to the Corinthians, "I planted, Apollos watered, but God

---

[17] We knew Avi and his wife, Leah, as "Al" and "Lois." They felt called by God to become citizens of the State of Israel in 1989 and took their Hebrew names. They enjoy dual citizenship there and in the United States to this day. Israel's Remnant was founded by Avi's father-in-law, and it eventually became part of a ministry called Friends of Israel. "Avi" is a nickname for Abraham (or Avraham), which was Avi's name at birth. Their son, David, is now the president of Jews for Jesus.

gave the growth."[18] My Inter-Varsity friends and mentors were among the finest Christians I have ever known.

But I also sought out unbelievers: people willing to state and defend their convictions *against* God. I wasn't so much looking for a fight, as I was wanting to try my worldview against theirs, hear their arguments, and attempt to answer them. I hoped I might be successful in persuading some to become Christians. I wasn't very good at it at first, but I kept trying. I found several brilliant, articulate fellow students who were willing to engage me and argue against everything I had come to believe about God. One especially stands out. I struck up a friendship with a man named Peter Thomas.[19] He was several years older than I, and he had taken time off from his classes at UConn to study with Britain's foremost "freethinker," the philosopher-mathematician, Bertrand Russell.

Russell was a formidable antagonist for any Christian and I wished I could meet him myself. I wanted to face up to the best the opposition had to offer. But getting to know and debate one of his devotees was the next best thing.

Russell's worldview was grim and fatalistic. In his most quoted statement, he summed it up this way:

> "… no fire, no heroism, no intensity of thought and feeling, can preserve an individual life beyond the grave… all the labors of the ages, all the devotion, all the inspiration, all the noonday brightness of human genius, are destined to extinction in the vast death of the solar system… the whole

---

[18] 1 Corinthians 3:6
[19] It only struck me years later how ironic (or perhaps appropriate) a name that was: "Peter," whose faith failed when Jesus was arrested, and "Thomas" nicknamed "the Doubter" when he refused to believe the other apostles when they claimed to have met the risen Christ.

temple of Man's achievement must inevitably be buried beneath the débris of a universe in ruins...."[20]

Peter Thomas shared Russell's worldview. I found it cold and depressing, but Peter was an intriguing person. I tried some of my best arguments on him.

- If the universe is ultimately "destined to extinction," and has no meaning...what does it mean to *say* that it has no meaning?

- If good has no more intrinsic value than evil, how are value judgments even possible?

- If in all our experience things wind down and fall apart,[21] how can we account for the continuing existence of the universe if there is no Creator God behind it?

Peter found none of this persuasive, but he appreciated my reaching out to him in genuine friendship. He was a loner, without many friends on campus, and eventually he went to live in Norway where he found the culture more congenial. But as my first year in college unfolded, I found myself deeply confused. Partly I had to acknowledge that Peter and some of the others had done their homework. They had substantial, well-considered arguments for their positions, and they were often better than I was at making their "case." They had a long list of serious questions that demanded better answers than I could give.

- If God is all-good, all-knowing, and all-powerful, how can there be evil in the world? If he's all-good, he's against it. If

---

[20]"A Free Man's Worship," first published in 1903 as "*The* Free Man's Worship." This remains Russell's best-known and most frequently republished essay.
[21]This is the simplest paraphrase of the Second Law of Thermodynamics.

- he's all-knowing, he's aware of it. If he's all-powerful, he can eliminate it. So, how did evil creep in?

- If Jesus is the only way to God, what about all the millions of people who have never even heard of him? How can a good God send them to hell?

- If everything is based on the Bible, how do you know it is accurate? Isn't it full of errors and contradictions?

These and so many other questions deeply challenged my convictions.[22]

At the same time, I found myself questioning some of the assumptions I had picked up as a young Christian. Most of my friends in the Bible Club and now those in the IV chapter came from churches holding restrictive views of drinking, smoking, dancing, women's makeup and skirt length, movies, and doing anything on Sundays other than going to church. No one ever tried to convince me these things were wrong, but a strong prejudice against them was part of the belief system of many of my friends, and it seemed to be part of the Christian package. I had accepted it uncritically, but now I began to have serious doubts about it.

My grudging respect for my non-Christian friends was growing just as my confidence in the cultural assumptions of so many of my Christian friends was slipping away. By the time summer break rolled around, I was deeply conflicted. It had all seemed so real just a year ago. I thought God had spoken to me; I thought he had become part of my life. Had I simply convinced myself of something I wanted to believe? I had thought I was going

---

[22] I have spent my entire adult life researching such questions. My friend, Tom Schach, has digitized the teachings I have given about them over the past 45 years, and made them available free-of-charge at www.BibleBanquet.com.

off to college to win the world for Christ. Now I was finding the world was forcing me to take a second look. I wrote a note telling my roommate, Ken, I was stepping down as Secretary-Treasurer of the IVCF chapter. "I'm happy to continue rooming with you, but I'm questioning where I am with the Lord, and I can't continue in leadership." Ken accepted my resignation.

But, when I returned to campus, I decided to attend the first meeting of the year – with extremely mixed motives. I was curious. I wanted to see what Ken would say about my resignation. And I expected to feel superior; after all, I was *taking seriously* questions my Inter-Varsity friends weren't even asking. It didn't seem to me they were even aware of them. I was in every sense, a "sophomore."[23] I went to the meeting feeling aloof, sophisticated, arrogant, condescending. ("The world is so much more complicated than most of you realize.")

And that's when I hit the wall.

God showed up. He was real. He was inhabiting the praises of his people. There was no question that he was in our midst, no question that these students knew him. They were singing about Someone they loved and trusted. The thing that had so attracted me to Miriam Beath, Howard and Ruth Wood, the kids in the Bible Club, Jimmy Johnson, Billy Graham, D.L. Moody, and so many other heroes of the faith was once again right in front of me. And it simply didn't matter how many unanswerable questions danced in my mind. Or how cool my unbelieving friends were. I remembered something Pastor Wood had said: "A man with an experience is never at the mercy of a man with an argument."

There is a fascinating detail in St. John's account of Jesus being arrested. He says that Jesus, knowing all that was to happen to

---

[23]The word "sophomore" is a compound word from the Greek, *sophos*, meaning wise, and *moros*, meaning foolish. A sophomore is literally "a wise fool."

him, came forward and asked the little band of soldiers, priests, and Pharisees, "Whom are you looking for?" They answered, "Jesus of Nazareth." And when he replied, "I am he," *they stepped back and fell to the ground.* (John 18:4-6) Most contemporary translations have a footnote on the passage. In the Greek original, Jesus' answer was simply "I am." He not only identified himself as the one they were seeking, but he did so by taking the unspeakably holy name of God upon himself and asserting his deity. And in the moment he did that, the reality of his identity was so overwhelming that those who had come to arrest him, could not stand.[24] I knew, in that first meeting of the year of the University of Connecticut chapter of the Inter-Varsity Christian Fellowship, that I was in the presence of the I AM God.

And suddenly it was *much* more complicated than that!

Seated directly in front of me was a young woman I had not met previously. We introduced ourselves briefly just before the meeting began. Her name was Karen Elvgren; as I later learned, she was the daughter of the popular artist, Gil Elvgren.[25] She had graduated from Ohio Wesleyan University the previous spring and had come to UConn on a three-year full tuition/room/board National Defense Act Scholarship to get her PhD in International Relations and Political Science.

She was beautiful. Obviously. Very. Bright. A scholar. Older than most of the other students in the meeting. And she plunged into

---

[24]Many people, including Jesus, often used the phrase "I am" without it referring to the YHWH name of God. But in the seven "I am" claims of Jesus (the Good Shepherd, the Bread of Life, the Door of the Sheepfold, etc.) and in at least three key passages in the Gospel of John, the phrase is clearly an assertion of Jesus' divinity. In John 6:19-20, 8:58, and here Jesus claimed his identity with the God of Israel.

[25]Gillette A. Elvgren (1948-1980). Gil did story illustrations for magazines like the *Saturday Evening Post*, advertisements, portraits, and landscapes, but he was best known for his pinups during and after World War II. At some point he was nicknamed "the Norman Rockwell of Cheesecake."

the worship with great enthusiasm. I was intrigued and attracted to her in every way. But *that's* not what I came to the meeting for! As the meeting ended, I found myself wanting to get to know her and understand her faith. I wanted to share my questions with her. Would she find them as unsettling as I did, or could she possibly have answers to some of them? I was way over my head! She was a grad student, and I was in my second year of college. She was 23; I was not quite 19. I would never have guessed that was both the beginning of the renewal of my faith…*and* a life-long love affair.

The next two weeks were a blur of confusion. I knew I was seeing again the thing that had most attracted me from my earliest visit to Sunday School at age three: the reality of the living God in the lives of people who know him. Here it was, again, in my Inter-Varsity friends. And here it was in Karen. It was undeniable.

And yet my friendships with unbelievers had raised so many intellectual questions and doubts for me. And I thought that most of my Inter-Varsity friends hadn't even wrestled with many of these questions. How could I respect their beliefs if they hadn't addressed the issues? Finally, I invited roommate Ken to spend a weekend with me in Old Saybrook. I hurled at him every objection to the Gospel that I had picked up - even some I already knew how to answer. He refused to argue. He simply said, "I know that I know that I know."

I remembered one of the songs we used to sing in the Bible Club. Each verse began with the phrase, "I know not how…" (or why, or what, or when). But then came the chorus:

> "But I know whom I have believed, and am persuaded that he is able
> To keep that which I've committed unto him against that day."[26]

---

[26]"I Know Whom I Have Believed," Daniel W. Whittle, pub. 1883, based on 2 Timothy 1:12 and Jude 1:24

Yes, it said, there *are* so many questions that are not easy. Some of them we may never be able to answer. But the issue isn't knowing *answers* but knowing *him*. The thing I had sought all my life was staring me in the face. God is real. Jesus is real. The Gospel is true. You can bet your life on it.

And I gave up. For the second time. Once again, I knelt by my bed. I begged his forgiveness for the presumption of thinking I was too smart to believe.

"Lord Jesus, forgive me for thinking I could handle all the arguments against you. Forgive me for putting so much trust in my own intellectual prowess. Forgive me for taking my eyes off you and looking instead at arguments about you. Forgive me for thinking of myself as being superior concerning the restrictions some of my friends accept. Lord, I cannot accept all those restrictions myself, but I am ashamed that I've looked down upon those who have done so. I know I cannot be the kind of Christian I was, but Lord, I want to be the kind of Christian you want me to be. Come, Lord Jesus, fill me with your Spirit all over again. Amen."

His love washed over me like a cleansing, healing bath. It was like being born all over again…again. I was eager to return to campus and tell Karen about the weekend. She was reluctant to believe it at first. But as I shared my heart with her, she saw that God had done something truly wonderful in me. And she rejoiced that she had been part of it. We began having "coffee dates" two or three times a week. I was rapidly falling in love with her. I loved her for herself *and* for her love for Jesus. She had a maturity in him that most of my other Christian friends lacked. I loved being around her and I loved talking with her about the Lord. And praying to him with her. She was both flattered and more than a little amused. I knew she enjoyed my company, but she didn't seem to take this undergraduate very seriously. She was dating a fellow grad student, but mainly she was just into her studies. Still, we had our Inter-Varsity meetings and two or three "coffee dates" each week.

I had joined the Air Force Reserve Officer Training Corps (ROTC). The annual Military Ball was scheduled for November, and I asked Karen to go with me, and to come meet my parents in Glastonbury afterward. It became the turning point in our relationship. Karen was taking things more seriously than I realized, and she had decided that if my folks seemed to like her, she would take it as a sign from the Lord that it was OKAY to pursue our relationship. "And, if they don't like me? I will end it, nip it in the bud." She didn't anticipate my parents' Yankee reserve! They seemed distant and aloof to her. She tells this story from her perspective in her memoir, *Planted by the River of Life* (2021): "It was apparent that his folks did *not* like the idea of their son dating an 'older woman'." And on the way back to UConn, she broke up with me.

I was devastated. My hopes for the evening had been so high: that everybody would be delighted with each other, and my folks would give their tacit approval to what was happening. Now it was dashed to the ground. I couldn't sleep that night. The next day was Sunday. I was distraught, and I skipped church. I decided to have a late lunch at a campus restaurant I had never tried previously. It was below ground level, down a long set of stairs.

Meanwhile, Karen (I learned later) was as undone as I was by her decision the night before. She expected to know God's peace, as she thought she was following his lead. Instead, she was deeply distressed, and she wept through church. She usually spent her Sunday afternoons reading to a blind friend named Sharon. She was doing that on this Sunday when she sensed someone approaching. Only, when she looked around, no one was there. Then, a hand seemed to touch her arm. But, again, no one was near them. She said, "Sharon, I know this sounds weird, but I think God wants me to go somewhere. Do you want to go with me?" Sharon said, "Sure; let's go!" And, with Sharon holding her elbow, Karen felt *led* by an unseen Presence out of the park, left, across the street, and down a stairwell to the very restaurant where I was just picking up my lunch, at about 2 o'clock in the afternoon - in a restaurant she had never previously visited, either. She entered the place just as I was carrying my lunch tray in front of her.

Astonished, we looked at each other, and she said, "It's OKAY. God brought me here to find you." I don't know which of us was the more bewildered. I went from despair to excitement; Karen went from thinking God was saying NO to our relationship, to beginning to believe he was saying YES...despite what my parents thought about it.

We were amazed. But we both needed even clearer guidance. Over the next month and a half, we enjoyed our deepening relationship. Then came Christmas break, and we returned to our respective homes: Karen to Sarasota, Florida, me to Glastonbury. One night, just after Christmas, I was reading the Psalms, and I came to a passage I had memorized some time before:

"Whom have I in heaven but thee? And there is *none* upon earth that I desire beside thee." (Ps. 78:25, KJV)

I suddenly came to a halt in my prayers. I could not say that verse any longer. There *was* someone on earth that I desired besides God. My return to the Lord was in part because of Karen, and I felt he had been blessing our relationship, but now I needed to know with certainty that this *was* his will for us. I knew I had to be willing to let it go if this was *not* his will. And I wrestled with him, with myself, and with that necessity for most of the night.

Getting to the point of being willing to walk away was a lot more easily said than done! But, at last, there was a breakthrough. I suddenly knew that if the Lord were to say, "This is *not* my path for you, John. You need to give Karen up," I could do so. No question that it wouldn't be easy, but finally I could say, "Not my will, but yours." And, the moment that happened, I sensed God saying, "I'm giving her back to you." It felt to me a little like Abraham's willingness to sacrifice Isaac, and finding God had a ram in the thicket instead. When Abraham was willing to give up his son, God gave that son back to him.[27] I couldn't wait to tell Karen about it the next morning.

She called me before I could call her. "I have to tell you what just happened," she said. But I insisted that I should go first, and I shared the story of my struggle and release, and God's reassurance. Then she told me that on the very same night, at the same hour of the night, she had been pondering our relationship, struggling to understand what God wanted for us, then she had a vision – her first. Here is how she tells it:

> "I saw myself sitting and staring happily at the sun, and then someone walked in front of me, and the light was cut off; I was in shadow… God gave me a clear word concerning
>
> what it meant for me: '*If your eye is single, your body will be full of light. But if your eye is not single, your body will be full of darkness.*' (Matthew 6:22-23, KJV)
>
> "Although I didn't recall ever reading this verse, I knew immediately what it meant for me: clearly someone – John Howe – had come between me and my focus on the Lord, and that is why I was suffering such mental and emotional darkness and confusion. I knew what this meant, and with considerable agony of spirit I relinquished my relationship with him."

---

[27] The story is told in Genesis 22.

We "gave each other up" at exactly the same time when we were twelve hundred miles apart. But while I had reassurance from God immediately, Karen's came a bit later. She went to a church healing service early the next morning, and the pastor – with no knowledge at all of what she was wrestling with – prayed for her: "May you be a clear and uncluttered vessel of the Holy Spirit." As he said that she felt an electric shock go through her body, and she heard the Lord speaking to her in an audible voice, *"It is my will for you to marry John, and you are to marry him within a year."*

Gasp! "How is *that* possible? John is just a sophomore; he's just turned nineteen. We are both full-time students. How can we afford a car, let alone an apartment? How can we afford groceries, utilities, insurance?" We made a list of things that would have to happen were we to be married, chief among them resolving her degree program. She was already having doubts about completing a doctorate, and if we were to be married, she would almost certainly have to become the principal breadwinner for the first few years. But she couldn't simply drop her scholarship.

The Lord began putting the pieces together. A student who had completed one year of the same National Defense Act fellowship at another school applied to transfer to UConn, and the Political Science Department was able to transfer what remained of Karen's program to him. Meanwhile, though she had not planned for it, she discovered that the classes she had already completed fulfilled exactly the requirements for a Master's degree.

Jobs opened up for both of us. I became a swimming instructor in the UConn athletic department and got an afternoon job in one of the grocery stores off campus. Karen was offered a position in the Acquisitions Department in the Wilbur Cross Library. Her dad gave us money for a car, and my father introduced me to a friend of his who ran a Chevy dealership who found us a very serviceable seven-year-old Bel Air. One of Karen's friends told her she was leaving school, and her apartment would be available in September: a rustic pine-paneled duplex just a couple of miles off campus. It reminded me of the home Gram and Poppy had lived in so many years before.

Karen wrote me a letter. The pages are yellow and brittle now, but I re-read it every so often. It is one of my most prized possessions. Here is what it said, in part:

Dearest John,

I didn't expect it to be quite like this – still and tempered and full of wonder. That's because I was expecting it to be emotional, and it isn't at all. It's just "knowing" in a secret way something too wonderful to dare to explore fully just yet...I'm letting the Lord reveal it tenderly, bit by bit.

The Lord made you and me to belong to each other. That doesn't mean we FEEL anything particularly intense and exciting and demanding...it simply means that together in the Lord we are intended to belong to each other, for his glory....

You're part of me, and I'm part of you! There's no effort at all, it's just a fact to be enjoyed and to be acted upon by believing he will prove our union by using us as one....

I never knew how much I needed my other half until I found you. Suddenly you aren't a third interest, along with my schoolwork and my ministry for him. We are part of each other, and therefore – together – we make time for whatever jobs we have to do, and we do it in him.

I love you and await the moment when I can give you this.

Karen

Following that terrible spiritual collapse, the Lord graciously restored me not only to himself, but to my roommate, Ken, and to our Inter-Varsity chapter. And that year the chapter elected me president.[28] But there was still the question of my education and career. I reflected that following Peter's denial that he even knew Jesus, the Lord not only restored him, but he renewed his calling. "Peter, do you love me?' "Yes, Lord, you know I love you." "Feed my sheep." I sensed that God still had ministry in store for me, as well. Would I be an English teacher, and run some kind of Bible Club as Ruth Wood had done? Would I be a Chaplain - or a Chaplain's Assistant – in the Air Force?

During that second year at UConn, I took a couple of courses in philosophy, and I was hooked. I was fascinated by the huge questions that have been argued by great thinkers down through the ages. And I still am. Whatever ministry I had would include wrestling with the thorny issues.

One of my professors was Joel Kupperman, earlier known for his appearances on the 1950s television show *Quiz Kids*. Kupperman was a child prodigy who astonished audiences with his ability to solve complex mathematical problems "in his head." In one episode he demonstrated his ability to quickly multiply any number by 99. When asked how he did this, he replied, "I multiply the number by 100, then subtract the original number from the total." I remembered seeing Joel on TV about a decade earlier when he was asked who built the Hanging Gardens of Babylon. (And, as an eight-year-old, I happened to know the answer: King Nebuchadnezzar II.) Joel was only six years older than I, so friendship was easy, and I especially enjoyed sparing with him in a course on political philosophy.

---

[28] I ran into a disturbing policy at UConn. "Religious" groups could hold their meetings off campus (as Inter-Varsity did, at the Storrs Congregational Church). But they could not hold on-campus meetings. I successfully challenged and reversed that policy with the help of the Young Conservatives group on campus.

But my favorite prof was Thomas Foster Lindley.[29] It was only after I had taken several courses with him that I discovered he had been a Methodist pastor before earning his doctorate in philosophy at Boston University. As our friendship developed, Dr. Lindley shared with me that he left the ministry because he felt he never found an adequate answer to the philosophical problem of evil.

Lindley said he had tried so often to comfort and care for parishioners who suffered illness, accidents, bereavement, hardship, loss – any of the myriad trials of this life – and he found his answers falling short both emotionally and intellectually. He never lost his faith in God, but he retreated from pastoral care into the realm of ideas and arguments.

I have been wrestling with the philosophical questions of pain, suffering, natural and moral evil ever since high school, and they remain some of the most sensitive points of contact with people facing crises (which, of course, is just about everyone at some point). I am convinced God never allows what we experience as "evil" into anyone's life without accompanying it with a redemptive purpose. As Joseph said to his own brothers who had sold him into slavery many years previously, "Even though you intended to do harm to me, God intended it for good." (Genesis 50:20)[30]

Somehow that wasn't enough for Dr. Lindley, but he was, nonetheless, a wonderful instructor, with a great gift for making abstruse things simple. And, over the next three years, we became good friends. He became my Faculty Advisor, and he guided me through my senior Independent Study, exploring what Jesus meant

---

[29]Dr. Lindley used his middle name in personal relationships, and he usually published as "T. Foster Lindley."
[30]My teaching on the book of Job has become the most widely distributed of any of the sermons, teachings, or writings I have ever done. It is available at BibleBanquet.com in the first "Early Years" series, under Old Testament Teachings, #3 – "The Man for All Seasons."

when he said, "I am the truth." (John 14:6) My thesis was that if Truth – the truth about God, the truth about the universe, the truth about ourselves – had somehow become a person, the only way to finally and completely *know* the Truth had to be by knowing *him*. I think it was a fairly awkward attempt, but Dr. Lindley awarded it an "A."

Located across the street from the UConn campus, St. Mark's Episcopal Church is one of several local houses of worship. It had become my custom to visit there frequently, usually in the evenings when I could be alone with God – to think, pray, and reflect on scripture. One night I stopped in to pray about my developing relationship with Karen. A man was in the choir loft, playing the organ.

My initial impulse was to leave; I wanted to be alone with God. But I decided to just ignore the organist and go ahead with my prayers. I went forward and knelt at the communion rail. But as I tried to focus, a strange prompting came upon me; it felt like a command: "Go pray with that man." I tried to dismiss it, but it was insistent: "Go pray with that man." Some people do that sort of thing easily, but nothing like that had ever happened to me, and I did not want to comply. But I had to. I went up into the loft and waited until he finished the piece he was playing. "Would you pray with me?" "Of course," he replied.

Now what?

I didn't know what else to do, so I continued my prayers about Karen and the plans for our wedding. And when I finished, he said, "Amen."

We introduced ourselves to each other; his name was Stuart Anthony. He said he had graduated from UConn several years previously and was now working as a medical technician in the next town. He was taking lessons from the church organist, and she allowed him to practice in the evenings.

And that was it! Or so it seemed. I left the church wondering what in the world had just happened. "And what does Stuart make of it?" I wondered.

Two nights later I needed to pray about something else altogether. I had been asked to co-ordinate a one-day retreat the following Saturday for our Inter-Varsity group, and I was concerned that everything would go well. I entered the church, and there was Stuart, playing the organ again. Curious! I had been in that church two or three times nearly every week, and I had never seen him previously. Now here he was two times in a row. As I walked down the aisle, that same strange urging occurred again. God wanted me to speak to Stuart. This time it was much more specific.

I turned around and called up to him: "Stu, you're going on a retreat this weekend!"

He smiled, "A friend is coming from New York this weekend, so I won't be able to join you." I said, "Stu, your friend won't be able to come."

Where did THAT come from?

He replied, "If my friend can't make it, I'd be happy to go on your retreat."

The next night the phone rang. Of course, it was Stuart. "My friend just called, and he can't come this weekend. I'd love to go on the retreat." On the way to the conference center, Stu told me a little more about himself. Alarmingly, he said he was a spiritualist - one who tries to communicate with the dead. I thought, "What have I done in inviting him to join us!" Our speaker that day was our Chapter's former president, Cal Fox. He did an amazing job, beginning in Genesis and ending in Revelation, and spelling out with great winsomeness and clarity the good news of the Gospel, our need and God's provision.

Toward the end of the afternoon, Cal asked if anyone would care to share any particulars regarding their journeys with the Lord. There was a brief silence, then Stu said, "I guess I'm the newest, so I'll go first." He said that during the break he had gone for a walk with Cal who had just led him to the Lord. And it was about to become even more astonishing. A week later I got a call from him. "I have been praying incessantly about what the Lord would have me do with my life," he said. "If Jesus Christ has done so much for me, what can I do for him in return? Tonight, on the way home, he spoke to me. He's calling me to become a medical missionary."

A medical missionary? A week ago, he wasn't even a Christian!

Stu said he had no family responsibilities to stand in the way, and he had accumulated sufficient savings. He resigned his job and enrolled in a three-year course of studies at Columbia Bible College, got ordained by the Baptists, and headed off to the jungles of Peru, where he spent the next thirty years of his life serving as a medical missionary with Wycliffe Bible Translators.

Months later he told me that on the night when we met and I asked him to pray with me, he had gone home feeling God was beginning something strange and wonderful in his life. He found his mother's Bible and opened it at random. His eye fell upon a verse that made his heart race: "*There was a man sent from God, whose name was John.*" He said he knew God was dealing with him! And everything else unfolded from that. Yielding to Jesus a few days later seemed nearly foreordained.

A few months later Stu was the Best Man at our wedding.

I spent the summer of 1962 in Glastonbury, working as a lifeguard and swim instructor at the Grange Pool, as I had done the previous year. Karen was at her parents' home in Sarasota, Florida, preparing for our wedding in September. My plan was to drive down at the end of August, in the car we purchased with the money from her dad and stay with the Elvgrens for a week before the wedding. Then for our honeymoon, we would take a leisurely road trip back up the east coast, with several stops along our way to Connecticut. But first came the wedding itself.

Although Karen had been raised Episcopalian, God used the Baptists to bring her into a living relationship with Jesus, just as he had with me. She had joined the Southside Baptist Church in Sarasota, where J. Roy Crosby was the Pastor. Although both of our parents were Episcopalians, it would be a Baptist wedding. Pastor Crosby counseled us beforehand, and reminded us in his brief homily, during the wedding itself, that we were beginning a great adventure together, and he included both a wonderful promise and a solemn warning:

> "If the vows you are making are remembered and faithfully discharged, they will add to the happiness of this life, lightening it by dividing its inevitable sorrows, and heightening it by doubling all its blessedness. But if these obligations are neglected and violated, you cannot escape the keenest misery, as well as the darkest guilt."

"Lightening and heightening," or "misery and guilt." So simple. The promise, and the warning, of every marriage. Our wedding party was fairly small. Karen's friend Janet Rae was her

Maid-of-Honor, and my two sisters, Sherry and Linda were her bridesmaids. Karen's brothers, Gil and Drake, were groomsmen and ushers along with Gary Molgard, a friend from UConn. And, of course, Stu Anthony was my Best Man. September first in Sarasota can be very warm, but the weather was lovely. And a funny little incident accompanied our festivities:

    I knew Karen's two brothers (and, as it turned out, her father) were determined to decorate our car. And I was equally determined that would never happen. I thought I had the perfect plan. On the morning of the wedding, I would park right in front of the house, where I could keep an eye on the car until everyone else had left for the church. Then Stu would come by (in his car) and follow me (in my car) to *another* church, where we would leave my car in the parking lot until after the reception. Then, Stu and Gary would go, retrieve my car from the lot, and Karen and I would be off. Who would think of looking for our car in the parking lot of another church? On the day of the wedding the Elvgrens left one by one, Karen and her parents to do last-minute preparations in the Bridal Room at Southside, Gil and Drake to begin their work of ushering. Shortly, Stu arrived.

    My car had not been touched. There was not a single decoration on it. I climbed in and chuckled as I turned the key…. Nothing. I tried two or three more times. Still nothing. I hadn't learned very much about auto mechanics during my brief time at Midway Garage, but I immediately suspected that Gil or Drake had pulled the rotor from the distributor making starting the car impossible. And then I realized I could still have the last laugh. Karen's dad had hired a fellow to watch the property during the wedding, who happened to drive a '55 Chevy Bel Air identical to mine. "Charlie, may I take the rotor out of your distributor? When the reception is over, you'll get mine back from Karen's brothers." Charlie agreed! I took off my white tuxedo jacket, rolled up my sleeves and pulled Charlie's rotor from his distributor, put it into my distributor, and started the car. I was laughing all the way to the other church parking lot. And still suppressing a giggle as the wedding began.

At the reception, back at the Elvgrens,' after greeting all the guests, we enjoyed the extraordinary buffet Karen's folks had laid out, listened to the guitar music of the well-known "Quiet Man" Ronnie Holloman as he serenaded my bride, and finally cut the cake. I asked Stu to go retrieve the car. When he returned with it 20 minutes later, it was decorated from top to bottom and end to end. It turned out that Karen's dad had asked the caterer to do the decorating during the ceremony. And as Stu and I were driving out, the caterer was just arriving. He said to himself: "That's the car I'm supposed to decorate!" And he followed us to the other church parking lot and did the job with time to spare before the reception began. Happily, his decorations were all in good taste. *Touché*, Elvgren men.

Obviously, marriage changed everything for both of us. But, as I reflect after six decades of sharing life with Karen, I'm amazed at how much it changed the trajectory she thought she was on. She had enrolled at UConn to earn a doctorate in political science and international relations. She expected to become a college professor or perhaps she would be involved in some form of governmental service. Instead, just a year later, she was a bride, helping her undergraduate husband finish his studies by working at the Wilbur Cross library.

There are often huge, unexpected changes in nearly everyone's life. I'm especially interested in how that happens in the lives of Christians who seek God's direction, who believe they have received it, and head off in one direction – only to then hear him saying something else altogether. How do we account for that?

I liken it to the captain of a ship, being given instructions to sail from point A to point B, but then, halfway to the destination, *new directions are given* to alter course, and head to point C instead. If point C was the real destination, why weren't they simply told to go directly there? *Perhaps because the Admiral giving directions knew there would be major problems in taking the direct route.* Perhaps there was a shoal, or a sandbank or rocks just beneath the water's surface that would have torn the ship apart had the captain tried to sail directly from point A to point C. The captain wouldn't see it on the surface, but the Admiral knew it was there. So, after setting off on the initial instructions, the captain receives a "mid-course correction" – a set of fresh instructions. He might not ever know why he was directed to zig-zag instead of going straight, but that doesn't matter so long as he is willing to change course when these new directions are given.

The Lord has seldom shown me (or most of the people I have known) the end from the beginning. He usually shows us just enough light on the path to take the first few steps. Then enough light for the next few steps. And so on. Often, we think we know our destination when we begin, only to have him tell us to make a turn somewhere along the way. How grateful I am for Karen's willingness to make that mid-course correction with me! What an adventure it has been ever since.

Our wedding was lovely, and it marked the beginning of our lifetime adventure together, but there was also an ominous note that we didn't learn about until sometime later. It was during our ceremony that my dad experienced the first tremors of what was eventually diagnosed as Multiple Sclerosis, "the great killer of young adults."[31] Over the final thirteen years of his life my dad

---

[31] Multiple Sclerosis is a disease of the central nervous system, in which the immune system attacks the protective sheath (myelin) covering nerve fibers, disrupting communication between the brain and the rest of the body. A patient suffering from MS may find various parts of the body becoming temporarily or permanently impaired – usually eyes, feet, and/or hands are initially affected. There may be periods of remission, but the most typical pattern is increasing

suffered increasing debilitation…until at last he put his trust in Jesus in a whole new way.

---

decline over time. Great strides in treatment have been made in recent years, but there is yet no cure.

Chapter 3

Preparing for Ministry

Study to show yourself approved unto God, a workman who does not need to be ashamed, rightly dividing the word of truth (2 Timothy 2:15).

Life with my bride was wonderful. We had a beautiful little apartment in a duplex a few miles off campus that we nicknamed "The Cottage Below" after the little chorus I had learned in the Bible Club:

> "I'm satisfied with just a cottage below, a little silver and a little gold,
> But in that City where the ransomed will shine, I'll have a gold mine that's silver-lined.
> I've got a mansion just over the hilltop in that dear land where we'll never grow old,
> And one day yonder we will never more wander but walk on streets that are purest gold."[32]

Karen and I rode together to and from school, she to the library, and I to my classes, studies and two jobs. Our rent was $95 per month, including utilities. Our budget for groceries and household items was $15 a week. I was still in Air Force ROTC, but I knew there was a call on my life from God going back to that night in Jimmy Johnson's Crusade. I wasn't sure that meant being ordained, but I thought I might be able to take an educational deferment, go to seminary, and serve in some capacity in the chaplain corps. I was also attracted to working with students, either

---

[32] *Mansion Over the Hilltop*, Ira Stanphill, 1949

at the high school or college level. (At that point I couldn't imagine being in parish ministry, let alone becoming a bishop!)

But, during my junior year, the Air Force eliminated educational deferments for seminary, and I had to decide. It was EITHER: go to seminary OR become an officer in the Air Force. I believed God was saying seminary. I was awarded the Medal of the Association of the United States Air Force during my junior year, and I have always partly wished I had been able to continue in military service. But the sense of call became overwhelming, and I asked to be released. I discovered I had to be court martialed! But it was a very easy process, and I was given an honorable discharge.

I applied to four seminaries, three of them theologically evangelical:

- The Conservative Baptist Seminary (now known as Denver Seminary), where Dr. Vernon Grounds was drawing together some of the leading Biblical theologians of the mid-Twentieth Century,

- Dallas Seminary, known for popularizing Free Grace Theology, and

- Gordon-Conwell Theological Seminary in Massachusetts, with the slogan "Think Theologically, Engage Globally, Live Biblically."

The fourth was much more mainstream and diverse: Yale Divinity School. I knew Yale would be a good deal more challenging both academically and spiritually, but I thought it would better prepare me for ministry in our rapidly changing culture. It was also a lot harder to get into Yale than any of the others. In Revelation 3:7, Jesus calls himself the one "who opens a door, and no one will shut it, who shuts a door, and no one will open it." Karen and I prayed that God would open the doors of his choosing and close all the others. To our surprise, he opened the doors at Yale, and for strange technicalities the doors at the other three schools stayed firmly shut.

I learned later that one of the factors in my acceptance at Yale was the unsolicited recommendation of John Perry, a friend from UConn who had gone on to YDS two years earlier. John and I were on the opposite ends of the theological spectrum, and we had often sparred in various meetings, but always with good humor and mutual respect. Those are the characteristics I have tried to maintain in dealing with disagreements whether theological, moral, or social.

When I first visited Yale, I wanted very much to meet one of its most distinguished professors, Dr. Kenneth Scott Latourette. "Uncle Ken" had begun his ministry as a missionary to China with the Student Volunteer Movement, but a severe case of amoebic dysentery forced his return to the United States. Latourette had joined the faculty of Yale Divinity School way back in 1921, and for the better portion of his time there he was the Chairman of Yale's Department of Religion, teaching Missions, World Christianity, and Oriental History. He had retired in 1953, but he continued writing and lecturing, and he hosted three different groups of students in his apartment each week: "Inter-Varsity types," married students, and a group of seminarians on scholarships from the Rockefeller Foundation who were there exploring whether they really had a call from God to fulltime ministry.

Latourette was a giant in his field, writing more than 80 books including his comprehensive seven-volume *A History of the Expansion of Christianity*. But he was also one of the humblest Christians I have ever met. The first time he welcomed me into his apartment, he greeted me with this self-introduction: "I'm a warm-hearted evangelical; I believe in the Virgin Birth." (Sad to say, many seminary professors don't!)

One of the last things I did before departing UConn for New Haven was to introduce Dr. Latourette to our Inter-Varsity Chapter. We asked him to speak about the beginnings of the Student Volunteer Movement, and the way it had transformed the world through Christian Missions in the Twentieth Century. He told us of a pivotal month-long conference sponsored by the great 19th century evangelist, Dwight M. Moody, in Northfield, Massachusetts in the summer of 1886. Its goal was to enlist 100 young men to volunteer for foreign missionary service.

He said this was such an important conference that one man, named John Raleigh Mott, a student at Cornell, in Ithica, New York, walked more than 300 miles each way from Ithica to Northfield to be there. "Uncle Ken" said that on the last day of the conference, as they headed into the final worship service, 99 young men had signed up, and just before the final benediction was delivered, the 100th volunteer stepped forward. John R. Mott was the best-known of those who did so. In later life, he helped found the YMCA, the World Student Christian Federation, and the World Council of Churches. He received the Nobel Peace Prize in 1946 for his work in establishing and strengthening international Protestant Christian student organizations that worked to promote peace.

It was amazing to think there was a thread connecting Dwight L. Moody, John R. Mott, Kenneth Scott Latourette, and me. Years later, when I became the Episcopal Bishop of Central Florida, I was intrigued to discover that John R. Mott had lived on the shore of Lake Eola in downtown Orlando, about a mile from my office. I often drove past it, reflecting on Mott's enormous contributions to the Church and to the culture.

"Uncle Ken" was fond of making the rigorous climb up New Haven's East Rock, a high embankment overlooking both the University and surrounding neighborhoods. I made that trek with him three times, and I had to push myself to keep up with this remarkable octogenarian. Though there were many ordained clergy among its faculty, Kenneth Latourette was the closest thing the Divinity School had to a Chaplain. And it was Dr. Latourette who was often called on when one of the undergraduate students needed a counselor.

My best friend in seminary, Jim Borchert, said he came to Yale as a believer, but he had no personal relationship with God until in the middle of a class on the Old Testament he found himself pondering the phrase "Vanity of vanities! All is vanity."[33] He said he suddenly saw his own life's meaninglessness, and when he bowed and asked Christ to make a difference…he did. Jim was the first – and only (!) – person I ever met who was converted through the book of Ecclesiastes. My years at Yale were rigorous, but wonderfully rewarding. When I told Dr. Jaroslav Pelikan, who taught the History of Doctrine, that I found his courses the most interesting of everything Yale offered, he said he was deeply surprised, but grateful.

Karen and I needed to determine our denominational affiliation. We were both raised as Episcopalians. We both had our faith awakened and we came into intimate personal relationships with Jesus through largely Baptist influences. We both had been deeply involved in the ecumenical ministry of Inter-Varsity Christian Fellowship. My "field work" at Yale involved joining the Inter-Varsity staff and visiting colleges and universities in southern New England. And, of course, Yale itself was an interdenominational school. So, were we to be Episcopalians? Baptists? Or something else? And, if something else, what? Two things helped us resolve that issue almost immediately.

---

[33] Ecclesiastes 1:2

First, we decided we would "church shop." We would begin with what was most familiar, our Episcopalian background. And if that wasn't a good "fit," we would "try out" different churches until we found one that was. Our search lasted exactly one Sunday. We attended New Haven's historic "Trinity on the Green" Episcopal Church. It is a building of great beauty, and the worship was comfortable and familiar. We walked in that first Sunday morning and somehow knew this was where we were supposed to be.[34]

The Rector was C. Lawson Willard, who greeted us warmly and asked if he could visit later in the week. Yes, we would be delighted! When he arrived at our small apartment on Canner Street, we told him our story, and shared both our sense of calling from God and our uncertainty about ordination. "Of course you will be ordained!" he said, "And of course it will be in the Episcopal Church! But," he continued, "John Esquirol, the Bishop of Connecticut will never ordain a Yale graduate. He would insist you go to an Episcopal seminary. Let me send you up to New Hampshire, where Todd Hall is the bishop. He's a Yale man himself, and he will take you on."

A couple of weeks later I was in Bishop Hall's office, and Willard was right. The bishop graciously offered me a place in the ordination process through the Diocese of New Hampshire. But it was on the condition that he would not have to "find a parish for me" after graduation. That was fine with me! I wasn't seeking a parish; I thought I would continue on Inter-Varsity staff after graduation. Bishop Hall said he would gladly ordain me as an Episcopal priest to continue that ministry.

I only met with Bishop Hall on three occasions: that first visit, a second time three years later, when I also took comprehensive "canonical exams" with the Standing Committee,

---

[34]Trinity was built between 1814 and 1815 and modified many times since. It was the first example of a Gothic style church building in North America.

and the third time, when he ordained me as a deacon on June 6, 1967 - during the Six Day War that was being fought in the Middle East.

On that day, half a world away, Israeli forces were surrounding the city of Jerusalem, and by noon it was clear that control of the ancient city was about to devolve to Jewish control for the first time since the Maccabean Revolt over twenty-one hundred years before.[35] Karen and I listened to the reports on the fighting as we traveled to and from New Hampshire.

Second, during our very first week in New Haven, we were paid a visit by the Rev. Peter C. Moore, a young Episcopal priest who had just become Director of the Council for Religion in Independent Schools (CHRIS). Peter said he had heard that an "evangelical Episcopalian" had come to Yale, and he simply wanted to stop by to encourage me. I never learned how he heard that, or from whom, but so began a lifelong friendship and partnership in the Gospel.

Peter wanted to reach prep school students for Christ using a model he had encountered in England. In his responsibilities as the Director of CHRIS, he visited private schools throughout the country, especially in New England, giving brief lectures in classes and sermons in chapel. He was a dynamic speaker, and students – and often faculty – would crowd around him with lots of questions whenever he gave a talk. He would then say, "You know, a group of students and collegians from all over New England are going to join

---

[35] Jerusalem fell to the Babylonians in 587-586 when Nebuchadnezzar II besieged the city and destroyed the First Temple, built by King Solomon three and a half centuries earlier. The Maccabean Revolt was a Jewish uprising against the Seleucid Empire led by Mattathias Maccabeus and his son Judas and lasting from 167-164 BC. Apart from that three-year period, Jerusalem had been under Gentile occupation and control for more than two and a half millennia. Jesus said that one of the signs his Return was drawing near was that "Jerusalem will be trampled on by the Gentiles, *until* the times of the Gentiles are fulfilled." (Luke 21:24)

me for a week of skiing and fellowship between Christmas and New Year's at a wonderful conference center near Mt. Sunapee. In the evenings we will gather around the fireplace and talk about some of the aspects of the Christian Faith that we've just been discussing. I'd love to have you join us."

At first, these "house parties," as he called them, attracted just a handful of students along with a few faculty and other adults. But as they became increasingly popular, Peter added spring/summer outings at the end of the school year.[36] We couldn't imagine how deeply intertwined our lives would become over the next few years. I would preach at Peter's wedding to Sandra Clark in 1968. A year later, Peter and Sandra would become godparents to our eldest daughter, Kathy.

At the end of my middle year at Yale, Peter invited Karen and me to a luncheon he was hosting on Long Island to introduce a large group of American Episcopalians to an Anglican missionary bishop from Australia named Alfred Stanway. "Alf" had gone to Africa as a young man with the Church Missionary Society, beginning his work in Kenya in 1937. In 1951 he was consecrated bishop of the Diocese of Central Tanganyika (now part of Tanzania), and for the next two decades he opened new congregations on the average of once a week. That's over 1,000 new congregations in twenty years!

---

[36]The very first such gathering was in the summer of 1961, and it included just nine boys meeting in a vacation home in the Adirondacks. During the first few years, "house parties" were separate gatherings for boys and girls, following the tradition Peter had encountered in Britain. As an organizational structure eventually developed, Peter gave it the name "Universities and Private Schools Camps," which was later changed to the "Fellowship of Christians in Universities and Schools" (FOCUS). The history of the first forty years of this ministry is told in *Be Thou Our Vision*, by Brooke Gunning and Molly O'Donovan, published by Gateway Press, Inc., 2001.

Alf emphasized giving leadership to indigenous Christians. Africans were trained and ordained. African bishops were consecrated. Alf supported medical and educational work, and he developed a network of Bible Schools. His emphasis on the value of Christian literature led to the development of book shops and the Central Tanganyika Press. He was a man of apostolic vision, tenacity, and faith. When he left Tanzania in 1971 his diocese was subdivided into five new dioceses. Peter Moore said, "You need to know such men are still around."

Several years later, in 1975, we would turn to Bishop Stanway, asking him to leave his retirement to become the first Dean/President of Trinity School for Ministry. He shared with us the four guiding principles of the Church Missionary Society on which he had built his work in Africa, and asked that we adopt them in founding TSM as well:

- <u>Begin Small</u>. We don't need to get everyone on board with a project before beginning. Begin with those who are ready to begin.

- <u>Trust God for the Vision</u>. We don't need to see the whole pathway to take the first few steps. God will shed more light on the path as we begin moving forward.

- <u>Put Money in a Secondary Place</u>. Money is important, but it is not all important. The question is not "Can we afford it?" but "What is God asking us to do?" And, most importantly,

- <u>Everything under God, depends on the Quality of the Person Selected for the Job</u>. The Bishop pointed out the high standards for the first deacons, even though their job was to wait on tables. (Acts 6:1-3) In the Old Testament, Bezalel was chosen to build the Tabernacle, not only because he was an extremely competent craftsman, but because he was also "filled with the Spirit of God." (Exodus 31:1-4)

Bishop Stanway was known for his "Alforisms[37]" – pithy statements of Christian wisdom hammered out in a lifetime of obedience, such as:

"God is a gentleman; he pays for what he orders." "If you are not willing to give away your best, God cannot bless you." "No Bible? No breakfast!"

In 1966 Peter invited us to participate in the December ski party in New Hampshire. We met at a wonderful old farmhouse converted into a conference center called Grey Ledges in Grantham, not far from Mt. Sunapee. Peter thought that with our Inter-Varsity connections we could be good liaisons to the college world for those who would be graduating the following spring. This was our first encounter with a significant number of prep school students. Karen and I were deeply impressed by the depth of the conversations that took place. These young men and women were intellectually much more like collegians than the high school students we had known previously. And yet they still had the same social needs and dynamics as other teenagers.

When the claims of Jesus were presented winsomely, in a way that respected both their minds and their hearts, many of them were eager to learn more. And many committed their lives to the Lord and began living for him. The opportunity to share biblical truth in a way that could change lives, in a fun social setting, was a great adventure. We went off to vigorous skiing at Mt. Sunapee during the day, then returned to a hearty meal in the evening, followed by zany skits and games. Then one of the leaders would give a brief talk on the claims of Christ, or the trustworthiness of the Bible, or the evidence for the resurrection, or God's provision of

---

[37] A play on his first name and the word "aphorism."

forgiveness, or the possibility of miracles, or the promises he gives for a wonderful joy-filled life, or any number of other elements of the Faith. Terrific conversations ensued, often late into the night. Many of the young people gave their lives to the Lord.

There was a funny incident on a New Year's Eve. A couple of us were talking with a student from Trinity College in Hartford. She seemed almost ready to commit her life to Jesus. "Why don't you just ask him to become your Lord?" I asked. "Okay," she said. Long pause… "O God…if you're really there…give me a sign…" At that very moment, the door opened and two of the Center's workmen brought in a huge billboard they were going to use as a dining table at the next day's festivities. Talk about a sign! My friend and I burst out laughing.

"You…don't…think…that…was…an…answer…to…prayer. Do you?" she asked. "You asked for a *sign!* Looks like you got one!" (She welcomed the new year and the Lord Jesus at the same time.)

Over the past 60 years, through the remarkable ministry of FOCUS, thousands of students have given their lives to Jesus, and hundreds of them have been ordained or otherwise become involved in some form of Christian ministry. I began to wonder if, instead of continuing on Inter-Varsity staff, there might be a place for me in prep school chaplaincy.

Chapter 4

Mixed Responses

When they heard Paul's preaching some scoffed; but others said, 'We will hear you again about this'...But some of them joined him and became believers (Acts 17:32-34).

In the spring term of my senior year at YDS, a small notice appeared on the bulletin board that The Loomis School in Windsor, Connecticut was looking for its next Chaplain. I decided to apply. A new Headmaster, Frederick G. Torrey, had just been appointed. We hit it off immediately, and he asked me to become Chaplain and Head of the Religion Department beginning in September 1967.

Graduation from YDS came first, followed by my ordination as a Deacon in New Hampshire on June 6, 1967. My ordination as a Priest came a year later, and it was John Esquirol, Bishop of Connecticut – the very one who "wouldn't ordain anyone who goes to Yale" – who actually ordained me, *on behalf of the Bishop of New Hampshire*, Todd Hall. Both of my sisters, Sherry and Linda, had become engaged to be married, and they asked me to perform their double wedding ceremony just one week later. Bishop Esquirol said, "You know, I've been a bishop for ten years, and I've never even been to a double wedding." I was just enough of a smart aleck to say, "Come next week, and I'll show you how to do it!"

The ceremony was unusual in more ways than just having two brides who were respectively each other's Maid and Matron of Honor.[38] By that time my dad used a walker with difficulty and was

---

[38] Sherry and Dave Cunningham were first to be pronounced husband and wife, and Linda was Sherry's Maid of Honor. Then it was Linda and Bob Albert's turn. By then, Sherry was already married, so she was Linda's Matron of Honor.

otherwise confined to a wheelchair with MS. We decided that rather than trying to have him escort either or both of his daughters down the aisle, their grooms would meet them at the back of the church and escort them in as well as out. Dad was seated at the front of the church, where he could proudly answer, "Her mother and I do" when I asked, first of one sister, then of the other, "Who gives this woman to be married to this man?"

Dad was obviously struggling with a kaleidoscope of emotions as he watched his little girls come down the aisle. It wasn't easy for me to begin the ceremony! "Dearly beloved: We have gathered together in the presence of God to witness and bless the joining together of this man and this woman…and this man and this woman… in Holy Matrimony…"

In the late 1960s most of the private independent ("prep") schools still had chaplains and required some kind of church or chapel attendance. Most seemed to think a little religion was a good thing…so long as it didn't go too far! The Loomis Institute originally educated both boys and girls, but in 1926 two separate schools devolved, Loomis for boys, and Chaffee for girls, and they were not reunited until 1970 as Loomis-Chaffee.[39] Both schools have had well-deserved reputations for academic excellence, but at the very point Fred Torrey invited me to sign on, Loomis was divesting itself of its remaining religious trappings. 15-minute Chapel services were scheduled on Mondays and Tuesdays, and a 15-minute Assembly, also held in the Chapel, on Fridays. The Friday Assemblies were nearly always secular in nature. Students were required to attend at least two of these three events, and to attend church on Sunday morning whenever they were on campus.

---

[39] The Loomis Institute was the product of great personal tragedy. The Loomis Institute was chartered in 1874 by five siblings who had lost all their children and selflessly determined to found a school for "all persons of the age of twelve years and upwards to twenty." Loomis-Chaffee today has a faculty of approximately 175, and a student body of more than 700 from 46 countries and 32 states.

I was responsible for all the above, doing most of the Chapel talks and church services myself; occasionally inviting other faculty or outside guest speakers, and scheduling most of the Friday speakers – usually other faculty or some of the students. Most of the boys put off their required attendance until Fridays, partly out of disdain for "religion," and partly because they put off nearly everything until the last possible moment. ("Who knows? The world might end before the week is over, and that will be one less thing I have to do!") I taught courses on the Bible, the history of Christianity, and World Religions. I also ran a tutorial project for indigenous students from Hartford.[40] In both the classroom and the Chapel, enticing the interest of the boys was always the challenge.

Karen and I became house parents in Batchelder Hall, with a two-bedroom apartment at the end of the second-floor corridor which housed about 20 senior boys. A doorway from our dining room led to their corridor and a set of back stairs, and we opened that door twice a week, inviting the boys to watch *Rowan and Martin's Laugh-In* with us on Monday nights, and *Mission Impossible*, on Saturdays. We would serve popcorn, chips, and soft drinks, and those were very popular times[41] I hosted a weekly Bible Study for anyone in the school who wished to attend. Usually about 6 or 7 boys showed up, and several of them gave their lives to Jesus. At least three of them went on to ordained ministry: Charlie Drew became pastor of Emmanuel Presbyterian Church in New York City, Scott O'Brien became rector of St. Martin in the Fields Episcopal Church in Chestnut Hill, Philadelphia, and. Neil Lebhar became a priest and then was elected the first bishop of the Gulf-Atlantic Diocese of the Anglican Church in North America.

---

[40]Robert, a fifth grader, came to the Loomis campus, and was deeply overwhelmed. He literally ran away from being involved in the project. I ran after him, tackled him, and held him tightly. After a few moments of struggling, he relaxed and then asked me, plaintively, "Will you be my tutor?" (Yes!)
[41]One day, as Karen was leaving the building via the back stairs, one of the boys jumped into her path, completely naked, throwing his arms wide open. Her response: "Oh, you cute little thing."

A few of the faculty also grew in their walk with the Lord during those Loomis days, perhaps most notably Dave Simpson, long-time French and Humanities teacher.

Sadly, while we were at Loomis my dad reached the low point in his battle with MS. My parents came for my birthday. Before dinner Dad tried to make it down the hall to the bathroom, using his walker, when his foot twisted beneath him, and he crumpled to the ground. I tried to prevent his fall, but I couldn't stop him. As he collapsed upon his own right leg he said, "Get me a gun." I'm pretty sure that, if I had done so, he would have used it. I had been studying the Book of Romans shortly before that terrible moment, and St. Paul's words in chapter five came flooding back to mind:

> "We boast in our sufferings, knowing that suffering produces endurance, and endurance produces character, and character produces hope, and hope does not disappoint us…" (Romans 5:3-5a)

I thought to myself: "God, are you mocking us? *My father is exhibiting the very opposite of what you have said!*" Instead of *endurance*, I'm seeing Dad's *impatience* – with himself, with his circumstances, even with the people around him. Instead of *character*, I'm seeing the *breakdown* of character. My dad, who had always been the strong, self-reliant, rock of our family was becoming increasingly petty, demanding, and critical – even and especially toward the very people he most depended on, my mother and my two younger sisters. And, instead of *hope*, I'm seeing *despair* – "Get me a gun."

But finally I realized: Paul wasn't writing about the suffering of *all* people! The key is in the next verse: "*…and hope does not disappoint us, because God's love has been poured into our hearts through the Holy Spirit that has been given to us.*" (5:5)

Paul was writing about the sufferings of *Christian* people who were trusting in the love of God. He was writing about those who have experienced the Spirit of God poured into their hearts. Dad was on the way, but he wasn't fully there yet. My father was one of the very best men I've ever known, and I shall ever be grateful for the early lessons he taught me. He was scrupulously honest, and he invested so much more of himself in me than I think many dads do with their sons. He had a life-long belief in God, but I don't think he really knew Jesus in a personal way…yet. When Dad was eventually hospitalized I asked my friend, Peter Marshall, Jr. to go with me to visit and pray for him. Peter was the son of Dr. Peter Marshall, Chaplain of the US Senate, whose wife, Catherine, wrote his story in the book, which was later made into the movie *A Man Called Peter.* Like his father, Peter Jr. was a Presbyterian minister who was known for his preaching and healing ministry.

Peter was very direct with my father: "John, I believe God wants to heal you, but not so you can go back to being the same man you've always been. He wants to make you a new person in Jesus. Are you ready to put your trust in him?" Dad said he was, and he prayed the "sinners' prayer." He still had much to work out (who doesn't?), but it was a new beginning.

Back at Loomis, I had a limited budget for the Sunday services. But I was able to bring in some remarkable speakers, including Yale's Chaplain, Bill Coffin whom I had gotten to know during my time in New Haven,[42] Gert Behanna, whose powerful personal testimony of deliverance from addiction to alcohol and materialism was heard by thousands of people in the early 1960s,[43] and Tom Skinner, the great African-American evangelist and former gang leader from Harlem. All three were very well received, as were

---

[42] Coffin became especially well known for his opposition to the Viet Nam War and his urging students to burn their draft cards.
[43] Gert's autobiography, *The Late Liz* (published pseudonymously under the name Elizabeth Burns in 1959 by Revell) was made into a major motion picture, starring Anne Baxter.

several others, but required attendance was still deeply resisted. Interestingly, I *favored* lifting the requirement, but not the way that happened.

During my second year at Loomis, just before Christmas, Loomis sponsored an evening lecture open to the public by the fiery community activist and political theorist Saul Alinsky, best known for his book, *Rules for Radicals*.[44] In the middle of his lecture about "taking on oppressive authoritarian structures," Alinsky made the comment that, "I got my start by boycotting compulsory chapel in college." The response was 100 per cent predictable. And unquestionably intended. The auditorium exploded with applause and shouting. It was several minutes before Alinsky could continue speaking. Alinsky had thrown gasoline on the smoldering coals of discontent, and he touched off a revolution. By the next day a majority of the students were demanding that Loomis drop its attendance requirement. And Loomis did.

There was a double irony here. First, most of the students appreciated the innovations I brought – changes in the worship style, the guest speakers I invited, etc. – but they hated being required to attend. Second, *I was on record* in favor of voluntary attendance even before Alinsky's visit, but now most of the hostility against "compulsory religion" was directed toward me. In a matter of days,

---

[44] Alinsky outlined eight steps for creating a socialist state: 1) Healthcare - control healthcare and control the people. 2) Poverty - increase the poverty level as high as possible; the poor are easier to control and will not resist if they are dependent on the state for everything. 3) Debt - increase the debt to an unsustainable level; then increase taxes and produce more poverty. 4) Gun control - remove people's ability to defend themselves from the government. 5) Welfare – take control of every aspect of peoples' lives (food, housing, income). 6) Education – take control of what people read and listen to; take control of what children learn in school. 7) Religion – remove belief in God from the government and the schools. 8) Class warfare – divide the people into the wealthy and the poor, thus causing greater discontent, and it will become easier to tax the wealthy with the support of the poor.

Loomis dropped all its requirements regarding Chapel and church, and I had to begin all over.

Up until that point worship at Loomis had been a kind of lowest-common-denominator congregational Protestantism. I began to incorporate a little more of the classic heritage of the church. I added a cross and candles to the holy table and began offering communion regularly. I continued doing most of the preaching myself, though we did still have guest speakers from time to time. As we moved into 1969 it looked like the chapel program at Loomis would survive.

Attendance at both church and chapel plummeted, but there were still enough students, faculty, and family members supporting the programs to keep them viable. And, because those who now attended *wanted* to be there, the atmosphere was hugely better than it had been previously. I continued sharing the Gospel, and we continued seeing both students and adults come to faith in Christ. One of the most effective ways of reaching the boys was having one of their fellow students who had come to know Christ share his testimony in our Chapel services. Charlie Drew gave a memorable chapel talk about how much he had craved the approval of others before he became a Christian, but once he found his security in Jesus, he was freed from concern about what others thought of him.

Three other big things happened in 1969.

First, our eldest child, Katherine, was born on February 24 in the Hartford Hospital. I had the joy of baptizing her at a FOCUS event the same weekend that a half million young people were headed to the Woodstock Music Festival in upstate New York. Karen and I began to discover, as every parent does, that we encounter the world all over again through the eyes of our children.

Second, very shortly after that, we found the first home that we actually owned – a tiny summertime cottage on the shore of Crystal Lake in Enfield, New Hampshire, not far from Grey Ledges, where FOCUS held its Christmas week house parties. It was a funny little house. The master bedroom was so narrow that our twin beds were on opposite walls, footboard to footboard, and the second story walls ended about a foot below the ceilings "to permit air flow". Household water came from the lake and drinking water from a spring behind the house that was pumped to our next-door neighbor's house, and from there to our house. He charged us $5.00 a year for that service. The house itself cost us all of $15,000 (!), most of which we paid from an inheritance from Karen's grandfather. It was a funny little place, but it was ours. We enjoyed the prep school vacations of 2 ½ weeks at Easter, 2 ½ weeks at Christmas, and 2 ½ months in the summer, and, though we only had it for three years, it was there that Karen and I wrote our first book (and the only one we have written together), *Which Way? A Guide for New Christians*.

In working with prep school students, we discovered that the same questions came up again and again: How do I know the Bible is true? How can I hear God speaking? How far should I go with sex? How can I share my faith? Etc. We were recommending (and in many cases, purchasing and giving away) about a dozen books to each of the students we were discipling. So, we determined to address these essential questions in a single volume of our own.[45]

New Hampshire winters are usually very cold, and our drafty little house had only a fireplace and a couple of space heaters. With both of them blasting away and a fire on the hearth, we managed to

---

[45] Young Life, a ministry to teenagers, purchased 10,000 copies, and distributed them across the country. In 2020, when I was received into the ministry of the Anglican Church in North America, I was greatly moved by Archbishop Foley Beach saying that he had been helped by studying our book when he was in Young Life as a teenager.

get the inside temperature up to a balmy 60 degrees. (We wore lots of layers.) And we had no running water in the winter, as the house was on pillars, with all the pipes exposed. I had to break through a thick cover of ice on the spring and haul water, but it was sort of an adventure. We purchased our first dog, an all-white Siberian Husky, whom we named Kiril, after the fictious Russian Pope in Morris West's *The Shoes of the Fisherman*. He was nearly indistinguishable from the white wolves pictured in the *National Geographic*, but he was extraordinarily gentle and protective toward Kathy. I tied a small beach chair on a Flexible Flyer sled, and Kiril would pull her through the snow and across the frozen lake.

When Kathy was two, we took her with us to a midnight service at a church in White River Junction, VT, where the rector, who happened to have a full beard, asked me to assist with the eucharist. Kathy was with Karen in the back pew, and when she saw us come out of the sacristy, dressed in our long robes, she exclaimed loudly, "Daddy!...and JESUS!" The whole congregation had a good laugh.

We had a ridiculous old hand-built boat with a 25 hp motor that was just strong enough to pull me waterskiing, with Karen piloting. I got pretty good at it, and when Kathy was just three years old, I began skiing with her in my arms as we took off in shallow water. Then, when I stood up on the skis, I told her to climb up and sit on my shoulders. She said, "Daddy, what if I fall?" and I – perhaps over-confidently – replied, "Do you think I would ever let you fall?" Fortunately, though we had many ski rides like that, I never did.

The third big thing that happened in 1969 was that Dr. Richard Davis, Headmaster of Miss Porter's School in Farmington, Connecticut, gave me a call. Miss Porter's was considering having a chaplain for the first time in its history.[46] Would I come talk with some of the faculty and students about what we were doing at Loomis? Of course.

Miss Porter's had always required its students to attend the church of their choice on Sunday mornings, but they were considering dropping that requirement. They wanted to explore the possibility of including religious instruction in the curriculum instead and providing on-campus worship. I told them what Loomis had just gone through, and we discussed what a possible curriculum might look like. (Bible, World Religions, Ethics, occasional guest speakers, etc.) I wasn't looking for a move, but the next thing I knew Dick Davis was asking me to become Miss Porter's first Chaplain. How amazing; the very things Loomis had just jettisoned Miss Porter's wanted to add! Karen and I prayed about it, and I said Yes.

I was to begin in September, but Dr. Davis asked me to speak to the school at a special assembly in May. I began by recounting one of my favorite episodes of Rod Serling's *The Twilight Zone* about a man who was sent to hell – only at first, he didn't realize where he was. Instead of fire and brimstone, he was in a kind of paradise in which his every wish was immediately fulfilled more wondrously than he could have imagined: plush surroundings, exotic foods, the finest wines, and more girls than he could count. (I said, "This vision might not appeal greatly to *you*, but I trust you can see how it appealed to *him*!") The episode continued: soon enough the novelty wore off, and he began to realize that the things he had longed for all his life were pointless: materialism without any meaning, popularity without purpose, sex without depth or love,

---

[46]Miss Porter's School was founded in 1843 by Sarah Porter, the sister of Noah Porter, former President of Yale College. Sarah was tutored by Yale professors, and she mastered four languages including Hebrew, which she learned in her eighties. MPS is perhaps best known as the school Jackie Kennedy Onassis attended (1944-1947), though Gloria Vanderbilt, Barbara Hutton, members of the Rockefeller family, and many other outstanding women were also students there, including Dr. Glenda Newell-Harris, the well-known internal medical physician.

power without value or virtue. *He was condemned to spend eternity amid the trivia of his own wish-fulfillment.*

I drew our attention to the person and the claims of Jesus: "I and the Father are one." "If you have seen me, you've seen the Father." "I've come to forgive your sins, restore your joy, and give you life forever with God." *Better to embark on the Impossible Dream in the fellowship of the Impossible Christ, than to spend eternity amid the trivia of your own wish-fulfillment.* To my utter astonishment there was a standing ovation! For a chapel talk! It continued for several minutes.

It felt like I was repeating St. Paul's experience in the book of Acts. There was an "uproar" in Thessalonica, but when he moved on to Beroea "they welcomed the message very eagerly…and many of them believed."[47] Of course, not everyone at Loomis had been hostile toward the Gospel, and not everyone at Miss Porter's embraced it. But the general responses of both students and faculty in the two schools could not have been more different.

In his *Chronicles of Narnia* series, when everyone's fortunes were about to change dramatically, C.S. Lewis said: "Aslan," – the great Lion King, the symbol of Jesus - "is on the move." Karen and I were very aware that Aslan was "on the move" as we prepared for our time in Farmington.

Dr. Davis asked me to put together a program for a two-day retreat to kick off the year in the fall. I invited the Rev. Peter Rodgers, recently ordained, who had been part of the FOCUS ministry, to come and give three talks. Peter recounted the life and career of King David, a mighty man of God in Old Testament days, but one who sinned greatly by committing adultery with his neighbor's wife, then having the neighbor killed in David's attempt to cover up the sin. Peter's bottom line was that, like David, we

---

[47]Acts 17:1-15

don't live up to God's highest and best, we *can't* live up to God's highest and best, and we *don't really want* to live up to God's highest and best. But he wants to become real to us, forgive that sin, and make us part of his forever family.

The response was amazing. The Spirit of God swept through the gathering. Most of the girls and some of the faculty were sobbing. Many said they "found God" that weekend, and others began a search for him. When Peter Moore heard about it, he said quietly, "Revival has come to Farmington." We returned to campus, but it was a different place. I began teaching several courses including Bible, Comparative Religion, and this time a course on Sexual Ethics. And this time there was great interest in exploring what for many was completely unfamiliar territory. I again hosted a weekly Bible Study in our living room that over the next three years grew to include nearly half the student body. After leading the study for two years myself, I began training some of the girls to lead Bible studies in their dorms. I wasn't trying to make them into great Bible *teachers*, but I simply shared with them how to *lead discussions* that enable small groups to get into a Bible passage and come to grips with its meaning and its application to our lives.[48]

Girls who had not been raised in church or Sunday School, and girls who were very new to the Christian Faith themselves, began leading wonderfully successful studies in their dorms, and discipleship multiplied all over campus simultaneously, like the chains of dominos that sometimes fall in many directions at once.

Karen and I were, again, dorm parents. We had an apartment on the first floor of an old three-story residence that also housed 41 senior girls upstairs. The weekly Bible Study was in our huge living

---

[48]Often called "inductive Bible Study," the leader asks three kinds of questions: what does the passage *say*? What does it *mean*? And what does it *mean to me*? (Observation, interpretation, application.) Inter-Varsity has produced a treasure-trove of helpful materials for doing this kind of study.

room, and my classes on the Bible, world religions, and ethics drew large numbers of students.

Karen joined me in the seminar on sexual ethics. We brought in a local doctor to help with some of the medical issues the seminar entailed. He was so pleased by what was happening with our girls that he arranged to fly us to San Francisco to address a national symposium of gynecologists on the topic of "communicating with young people about sexual morality."

I discovered that just as I was beginning my ministry at Miss Porter's, another Chaplain was beginning his ministry at Ethel Walker's, a neighboring girls' school in Simsbury, the next town over from Farmington. The Rev. Harald Haugan, known to all as "Whitey," became a great friend and partner in ministry. We were on the same page spiritually and theologically, and we began sharing teaching weekends and workshops. We were seeing such good things happening in both schools that I wrote an article for *Christianity Today* urging seminarians and others to consider private school chaplaincy as a venue for their ministry and a fruitful field for evangelism.[49] "Come over and help us," I said.

Teachers, coaches, and chaplains in preparatory schools – especially residential schools – have the responsibility and the privilege of playing critical roles in the lives of their students. They can function as big brothers and sisters, role models, and what the psychologist Erik Erikson used to call "adult guarantors", older friends who give young people the hope that their lives will eventually turn out well. Tragically, sometimes the parents of these students abdicate much of their own responsibility for helping their kids through their growing-up years. At Miss Porter's I had a couple visit who wanted to talk with me about their daughter. "We know she is unhappy," they said. "We are prepared to do anything for her." "What does that mean?" I asked. "Anything means anything. We

---

[49] *The Prep School Ministry*, Christianity Today, February 27, 1970

will buy her a car. She can take a year off, go the Riviera; anything." I had their daughter as one of my advisees. I said, "I happen to know that what she wants is to come home." "Oh, no," they said. "There's no place for her there. We like our life the way it is." I politely asked them to leave my office.

Early in our time in Farmington we learned of a wonderful and unusual church nearby called "The Barn." Officially it was the Covenant Presbyterian Church, but it was, literally, a barn. Its worship space was in what had been the hayloft, and its offices and meeting rooms were on the ground floor beneath it. Worship was on all four sides of a raised platform in the center of the loft, where the communion table was stationed beneath a full-size cross suspended from the ceiling. The large, diverse, joy-filled congregation welcomed the ministry of the Holy Spirit. Often there was fervent open prayer, and prophetic messages were shared by many of the worshippers. Occasionally there were messages in other languages, always followed by interpretation, in accordance with St. Paul's instructions in First Corinthians.[50] The services were dynamic, filled with the Holy Spirit, and many of the students from both of our schools decided to join Karen and me as we began to worship there regularly. I drove a school bus full of students to Sunday services, stopping at Ethel Walker's to add several girls from there. We always arrived early enough to sit in the front row.

The Barn had two pastors, John Hunn and John Bankowski. They were usually called "the two Johns." Both were gifted preachers, and they often presented dialogue sermons. One would begin, then after ten or twelve minutes the other continued, perhaps moving in a slightly different direction. And after another few minutes the first would summarize and conclude. But what often happened after the preaching was even more impressive. As the congregation sang quiet praise music, anyone desiring prayer was

---

[50]See chapters 12 – 14, especially.

invited to the central platform, where several trained and sensitive intercessors stood ready to come alongside those seeking prayer. Most of the intercessors would ask quietly what the petitioner wanted prayer for, then join him or her in bringing that request before the Lord. Often, the following week, there were testimonies that God had answered these prayers in dramatic, sometimes astonishing, ways. And occasionally we saw people healed before our eyes when they requested prayer.

John Bankowski had a different approach. He waited, praying silently, until the Holy Spirit directed him to someone who had come forward. Then, *without asking any questions,* Bankowski prayed over the person as the Spirit of God led him. Frequently some of the girls from Porter's would go for prayer, and I usually knew why - because they had shared with me about it earlier in the week. Repeatedly, when John Bankowski was the one praying, he would nail it perfectly. Without being told by the students – or by me – what was troubling them, he would pray for exactly that thing. In First Corinthians, St. Paul tells us that one of the gifts of the Holy Spirit is speaking a "word" or "utterance" of knowledge[51]. Speaking such a word is telling others things one couldn't know except by revelation from the Holy Spirit. It was a "word of knowledge" when Jesus told the woman at the well in Samaria "you've had five husbands, and you're not married to the man you're living with now."[52] Unless we think Jesus stopped by the courthouse and checked the records on his way into town, that had to be something the Spirit of God whispered to him in that moment. When I told Stu Anthony his friend in New York would not be coming the next weekend, so Stu could join us on our retreat, I was speaking such a word. John Bankowski manifested that gift Sunday after Sunday.

One Sunday Karen and I were on the receiving end. It was in our second year at Porter's, and sometimes our house-parenting

---

[51] 1 Corinthians 12:8
[52] John 4:18

responsibilities were wearisome. We had forty-one seniors living with us in the three-story Humphrey House on Farmington's Main Street. We loved them, but their endless interruptions and requests could feel excessive. "May I borrow this?" "Can you please sew this torn shirt for me?" "Can you lend me some money until Friday?" "Would you be able to drive me to...wherever?" And of course, it was the growing number of Christian girls, both in Humphrey and elsewhere, who asked most often! They thought – correctly – we had a special concern for them. But they were often thoughtless about what plans of ours they might be interrupting. When we went to bed one Saturday night, I said to Karen, "I am so tired of these kids asking, asking, asking. I really don't want to see any of them again for a very long while!"

When we got to The Barn the next morning, I glanced at the service leaflet. The scripture reading was to be 1 Peter 5:1-5. I knew that was Peter's exhortation to his fellow elders to "tend the flock of God that is in your care...not for sordid gain but eagerly." I said to Karen, "I suspect we're going to get it today." And we did. Both pastors spoke of the way all Christians, but especially Christian leaders, need to be generous givers of their time, their money, their love, and their care. We agreed we needed to go up for prayer. And who was it that came to pray for us but John Bankowski. He put a hand on each of our shoulders. And then...silence. His face was strangely contorted. Finally, he said, "Please know I can only pray as I am being led... There was a couple named Ananias and Sapphira, and they held back. And the Lord would say to you: *Do not hold back*."

The story of Ananias and Sapphira is told in chapter 5 of the Acts of the Apostles. Early in their history the first Christians tried an experiment in communal living. Everyone donated to a common treasury, and all expenses were paid from it. Although some have argued it was a model for all time, the experiment didn't last very long, and there is no Biblical instruction that it was to be continued. But Ananias and Sapphira *claimed* to have donated everything they had, while in fact they retained some of the proceeds from selling a piece of property. They "held back." And for that lie, God struck them both dead. Was Bankowski implying that my grumpy reaction to our demanding girls in Farmington was like the "holding back" of Ananias and Sapphira? Could our "holding back" lead to God striking us down, as well?

Whew! We certainly *did* get it that morning. Karen and I determined that from that time on – unless we had some prior commitment making it impossible – our answer to every request from the girls would be Yes. God knows our schedule; he knows our needs. And he can protect us. If he allows a student to come with a request, our job will be to meet that request unless it is simply not possible for us to do so. And, to the best of our ability, we lived out that commitment for the rest of our time in Farmington.

One day a young woman named Elise came knocking on our door. She said she had been living with her boyfriend at Trinity College in nearby Hartford, but he had kicked her out. Somehow, she heard that wonderful things were happening among the girls at Miss Porter's, and she came hoping we could help her out.

Of course, we said we would do whatever we could, and for the next several weeks she lived with us. We shared the Gospel with her, and she said she wanted to accept Jesus, but something was holding her back. We began to suspect there was a serious spiritual hindrance. Had she ever been involved in occult practices? Oh yes, she said her mother was a practicing witch (!) and Elise herself had experienced trances, telekinesis, and other magical phenomena. We prayed for her, but there was no breakthrough. She was deeply agitated, and there was neither joy nor liberty in her spirit. We shared our concerns with the two pastors at The Barn. They agreed that there could be some kind of demonic influence affecting Elise. They said they had not had much experience dealing with such things themselves, but there was a young couple in the congregation that had wonderful results in similar situations, and perhaps they could help.

So, we sought out George and Victoria Hobson.[53] We prayed together, and they agreed to meet with Elise and the two of us. We would counsel her, pray for her, and if we discerned the need, we would ask God to set her free from any spiritual oppression. We agreed we would fast beforehand.[54] Until then I had never spoken in tongues or seen a vision. (Karen had done both.) But as I prayed for Elise I said, "Lord Jesus, if one of the gifts of your Spirit would enable me to better help this young woman, please give it to me. If praying in tongues would help, let me pray in tongues. If seeing a vision or receiving a word of knowledge from you would help me minister to her, please make that happen, as well."

And I saw my first vision. It was simply a light at the end of a long, dark corridor. And I spoke a few words in a language I had never learned. (And, of course, I was immediately proud of having done so.)

We had a long, loving, prayerful time of ministry with Elise, and George did discern the need to command an evil spirit to depart. Elsie displayed no great external evidence, but suddenly she was at peace, and she exclaimed, "I'm free!" She was then able to commit her life to Jesus, and I baptized her in our living room. She has had

---

[53] George was a layman in 1974, having done his B.A. at Harvard. But, in the years since then he has completed his M.A. and PhD. at Oxford University. He was ordained in 1988, and in 1995 he became the Canon Theologian of the American Cathedral in Paris. He has published numerous books of theology and poetry.

[54] In the story of Jesus healing the epileptic boy, some authorities add the verse, "This kind does not come out except by prayer and fasting." (Matthew 17:21)

no relapses, and she is long-since a happily married wife and mother.

Several months later, as my father continued struggling with Multiple Sclerosis, I asked George and Victoria to visit my parents with us and pray for Dad. They discerned a strange phenomenon in him. Dad had experienced several deep disappointments in his life, perhaps the greatest being that his employer had called him back to Hartford after thirteen years in Illinois, with what seemed to be a promise they would make him an officer in the company. But, for whatever reason, they never did. Somehow, Dad had absorbed all these disappointments, on the surface at least, not allowing them to "hurt" him. But inside, he was deeply disappointed.

Neither the Hobsons nor the Howes are psychologists. But many medical experts have suggested a possible correlation between suppressed disappointment and MS. Whether or how disappointment might have affected my father, I don't know. But in our prayer that afternoon, George suggested that Dad needed to forgive people who had hurt him. And he did that. There was no physical improvement. But there was a change in Dad's spirit. As there had been with Elise, there was suddenly a release in Dad, and a new sense of peace came upon him. And in the next few weeks his pattern of criticizing and belittling others that had become so disturbing began to reverse.

One afternoon he asked to speak with me: "I pray every day that God will heal me of this damnable disease, but it doesn't look like he's going to do so. But I want you to know this. I have discovered what I should have known all along – that I'm completely dependent on him. And, as difficult as this condition is, it has been worth it, because Jesus alone is sufficient." In the closing months of his life, my father began studying for the ministry – with me as his tutor. We didn't get very far with his studies, but one day I'll see him again, and I suspect he will have gone far beyond where we left off.

In 1971 the graduation ceremonies at Miss Porter's were nearly cancelled. The night before graduation, parents (who came from around the world) took their daughters to the very best restaurants in the area to celebrate. Unfortunately, in too many cases there was too much alcohol for girls too young to handle it. Several of the seniors in our house came in late and in not-very-good condition. At about 11:30 PM, George, the campus policeman, told me he had just apprehended one of our girls drunkenly riding her bicycle down Main Street in her underwear. News of a great deal of inebriation reached the headmaster, and around midnight Dr. Davis phoned me saying he had decided to cancel all of the following day's activities.

I rounded up the student leaders of the school and asked them to compile an assessment of the pattern of student drinking during the past year. They produced a picture of multiple instances of faculty and staff – including the headmaster's wife – sharing wine with students on numerous occasions during the school year. At about 4 AM I went to Dr. Davis's home and presented their report, and said, "You really can't cancel things based on this past night's infractions. We need to address the larger pattern going forward, but for today, graduation must be observed." It was. And later on the drinking issue was properly addressed.

There was an extraordinary incident at the FOCUS house party on Christmas Eve in 1971.[55] Freezing rain had fallen on top of packed snow for most of the day. The weather finally lifted and some of the kids went out to sled and toboggan. The hilltop was solid ice. One of the girls slammed into a tree, bashing her head badly. She went into convulsions, screaming and flailing about. We got her into the building, but what could we do? The nearest hospital was about forty minutes away under normal conditions. This was

---

[55]I told this story previously in *Anointed by the Spirit*, Creation House, (2012), p. 79, but it bears repetition here.

New Year's Eve, and the roads were glare ice. Someone said, "Let's pray!" And I heard myself say something I had never said before. Instead of, "Oh God, please heal her," I said, "In the name of Jesus, be healed!" Her tears and convulsions stopped immediately, and a huge smile replaced them. She said, "Oh, I'm going to know him now!" I said, "You didn't?" "No," she said, "but I'm going to." She did. And she does.

Life at Miss Porter's seemed as wonderful as we could imagine. Students were committing themselves to Christ, Bible Studies were happening in the dormitories. The Bible Study in our apartment had grown to where we could hardly squeeze another person into the room. There was very little opposition to what was happening. We were developing a network of support among neighboring schools, especially Ethel Walker's. We were attending an amazing church on Sundays and bringing students with us. We had a lovely little lakeside home and a long summer vacation during which we could write books and articles and I could plan for the coming year's academic courses. We planned to be at our cottage in New Hampshire during Christmas break, which meant we could participate in the FOCUS house parties at nearby Grey Ledges. Our young daughter was a delight, we had a great dog, and life was wonderful in every way. But it was about to change for the Howe family again.

Chapter 5

A Call to Parish Ministry

I was not disobedient to the heavenly vision (Acts 26:19).

I had never met John Guest, but I knew of his reputation as a superb preacher and evangelist. Real evangelism was rare in the Episcopal Church. People often quip that Episcopalians are afraid of "the e-word." When challenged that we are commanded to share the gospel, Episcopalians will usually respond that they try to witness by their lifestyle. John Guest is different. He has often been called "the thinking man's Billy Graham." His sermons and talks are probing, thoughtful, challenging, and convincing. And they nearly always call people to commitment to Jesus.

Born in England, converted in a Billy Graham crusade, and ordained an Anglican, John had come to the United States under the auspices of Scripture Union, with a ministry focused primarily on college and university students in the Pittsburgh area. He played a twelve-string guitar, and traveled with a Christian rock band, called the Exkursions. And, to provide a home base, he had a part-time job as Youth Minister at St. Stephen's Episcopal Church in Sewickley, Pennsylvania. Timmy Nash, a student at Miss Porter's, was from Sewickley, a member of St. Stephen's, and she urged me to invite John to speak at one of our school assemblies. I did, and he said yes. John brought his guitar along and sang for us. He told stories and jokes. And then gave a wonderfully compelling talk about the claims of Christ. He was extremely well-received. And the two of us began a lifelong friendship.

A couple of months later John called me. "Something extraordinary has happened," he said. "St. Stephen's has asked me to become their rector. Would you pray about becoming my associate?" I agreed, this *was* extraordinary. In many ways, John was an unlikely choice. In keeping with his ministry to youth and college students, John wore his hair fashionably long. He usually dressed in bell-bottomed trousers, and compared to the retiring rector, he was a very young man. Sewickley is one of the toniest towns in America, and St. Stephen's one of the more sophisticated parishes in the Episcopal Church. Their Search Committee looked at candidates from all over the country, but each time they interviewed someone, or heard him preach, they said to each other, "He's not as good as John Guest." So, it was amazing that this young, evangelical, British youth minister was being asked to become the rector of a very prominent establishment church. And now he was asking me to become his Associate Rector.

"Wow! Thank you," I said. "But no; I'm where I should be." "Will you pray about it for a month?" "Well, sure." I didn't really pray about it very earnestly; I couldn't imagine God wanted me to do that. And when John called again, I turned him down a second time.

But then I began to have a nagging sense that I hadn't been fair to him. Or to the Lord.

I went across the street to a little Episcopal Church to seek God's clearer direction. I said, "Lord, I'm sorry that I haven't taken John's invitation more seriously, and if this is something you want me to accept, I ask you to speak in a very specific way. I'm going up to the Bible on the lectern, and I ask you to speak to me out of whatever passage it is open to just now." Opening the Bible and expecting God to speak from wherever it falls open is sometimes called the "Christopher Columbus Method" of studying the scriptures (sight and land). Karen has often gotten remarkably clear and on-target guidance that way. But usually when I have tried it, I have not seen any connection between the passage and whatever it was I was praying about.

This time was different. The lectern Bible was open to the passage in Isaiah where the Lord says to King Ahaz, "Ask a sign of the Lord God; let it be deep as Sheol or high as heaven." (Isaiah 7:10) That passage is often read during Advent, so I thought it was a bit odd to find it in early spring. But I said, "OKAY, Lord, if that's your invitation to me, here is the sign I request: Please have John Guest call me a third time and tell me I'm the only guy in the country he's interested in."

I went back to our apartment, and asked Karen, "What would you say if John Guest were to call me and tell me I'm the only guy in the country he's interested in?" She said, "Well, that's pretty conceited, isn't it!"[56] Twenty minutes later, the phone rang. And my life was changed forever. John used almost exactly the words I had requested in inviting me for the third time to become his Associate. Miss Porter's graciously released me from the contract I had already signed. We sold our beloved cottage in New Hampshire. We said goodbye to the girls we had grown to love so dearly. We thanked the two Johns at the Barn for their ministry to us and to our students. And we were off to Sewickley and a *completely* different life.

John Guest is a man of huge imagination. He generates ideas at an amazing rate, most of them excellent and challenging. Keeping up with him is often difficult. Several times I said, "John, we can't do everything at once." And he always replied, "Yes, but we have to do more than one thing at a time." We laugh at it now, but we have said that so often it has become almost our way of greeting each other. He was clearly the Rector, the senior pastor, and I was clearly the Associate or second-in-command. But John shared as much of

---

[56]Her actual words were slightly saltier than that, but she denies it.

the ministry and leadership with me as was possible. (I was brought up short, however, when I tried to call on one of the parish matriarchs living in Sewickley Heights. She sent word to the front door that "When *the Rector* decides to visit, I will be happy to see him.")

Nevertheless, John and I were very much on the same page. It often felt as if we could finish each other's sentences. On occasion we gave dialogue sermons, like the other "two Johns" at the Barn in Simsbury. Up until then I had seen myself as something of an evangelist. But John is so hugely gifted in that ministry that I began leaning more toward teaching, just to provide balance. I try to always have an evangelistic element in my preaching and teaching, but my emphasis is more on "rightly explaining the word of truth." (2 Timothy 2:15) I sometimes said, "John is a proclaimer, and I am an explainer."

It was a challenge and an honor to work with John Guest for the next three and a half years, and the Lord greatly blessed our ministry. The church grew numerically, spiritually, and financially. We were able to keep most of the congregation we inherited, while seeing God raise up a significantly younger generation alongside them. Karen and I, along with our 3 ½ year old daughter, Kathy, moved into the large colonial house (with picket fence!) on the corner, adjacent to St. Stephen's. It was far more house than we needed, but we were able to give Kathy a large playroom, where Karen painted wonderful murals of animals and fairies on the walls, and we turned a small room at the top of the stairs into a prayer room, where we each had our own prie-dieu (prayer desk). Living next to a large, prominent church on one of the major roads into Sewickley, we found we had many people stopping by our house hoping we could give them a meal or a handout. Many of them were genuinely needy, and we were eager to help. Some, unfortunately, seemed to be professional beggars, going from one church to the next getting as many "freebies" as they could. Many, of course, were also alcoholics.

We developed a standard way of dealing with them. In the St. Stephen's congregation there was a delightfully reformed hit man named Bill Moore, himself also a recovering alcoholic. Bill had lost his leg in some kind of criminal incident, and he wore a prosthesis. And he had tried to take his own life in a drunken rage, plunging an eight-inch kitchen knife into his chest and barely missing his heart. He awoke in the hospital and was about to try to rip his stitches out and finish the job, when he had a vision of Jesus, standing with his arms outstretched, and saying, "I died for you; you don't have to do that." Bill was converted on the spot, and never had another drop of alcohol. He became a schoolteacher, always eager to share his story with both kids and adults. Bill had a heart of melted marshmallow, but an exterior like tungsten.

Whenever someone came knocking on our door obviously having had too much to drink, Karen and I invited him in, gave him a good meal, and put him to bed in our guest room. Then I called Bill, who arrived minutes later. Bill would awaken our visitor with the words, "I'll give you two options: quality sobriety or a ride out of town." One fellow to whom he said that angrily replied, "You can't talk that way to me. I've been around!" Bill pulled open his shirt, showing his self-inflicted scars, then showed his prosthesis, and said, "I've been around, too. Now, which do you want, the ride or some help?" Most folks took the ride, but some gratefully accepted Bill's witness and ministry – which always included getting them into an AA meeting as soon as possible.

Most of the St. Stephen's family welcomed both John Guest's ministry and mine, but there was a pocket of opposition. Just before the annual meeting of the parish we learned that one of the hostile men in the congregation was running a campaign to get himself elected to the vestry. It was successful, and the morning after the meeting he arrived at the office to confront John and me. "I've been elected," he said, "and I have a mandate from the congregation to save this church from the two of you!" Making things infinitely worse was the fact that he was the husband of my secretary. Under any other circumstances, she should have resigned immediately, but I could not ask her to do so without it being called punitive. I decided to try a different approach.

"George," I said, "How about meeting with me once a week for breakfast? Let's take a look at some scripture together and share our thoughts and concerns." He agreed. The first few weeks were simply terrible. But we persisted. And slowly, painfully, we began to see each other's point of view on many key issues. That didn't mean either of us changed our minds about much, but we found we could appreciate the other's perspective. And we prayed together. Perfunctorily at first. It was painful, but as we persisted, we found we were praying with increasing sympathy for each other's concerns. George's business was struggling; I was happy to see things begin to improve as we asked for God's blessing. And over the next few months, we found ourselves beginning to truly become friends. I don't know which of us was the more surprised. By the time I left Sewickley, three and a half years later, George had become John Guest's right-hand man. When John hosted the first National Pastors' Renewal Conference, George handled all the administrative operations.

During our clergy meetings, John had a surprising practice of asking those present to remove our shoes. Then, as we continued our discussions, he would routinely shine them – reminiscent of Jesus washing his disciples' feet. We met for an overnight about every six weeks with a consortium of pastors from several of the most prominent churches in the Pittsburgh area along with the leaders of a few "parachurch" ministries such as Young Life, Alcoholics Anonymous, the Coalition for Christian Outreach, and the Pittsburgh Experiment.

The Pittsburgh Experiment was one of several ministries that began under the leadership of Dr. Sam Shoemaker when he was Rector of Calvary Episcopal Church in Pittsburgh. During the concerted campaign to revitalize the Steel City in the 1950s, Sam met with a group of the leaders of business and industry at the Duquesne Club and told them that "it takes more than renovating buildings to rejuvenate a city. It takes the renovation of human hearts." He challenged them to go on a month-long "Experiment" of involving God in the details of their personal and business lives. "Ask Jesus into the intimate details of your marriage, your finances, your business, and see what happens," he said. The results were so dramatic that the Pittsburgh Experiment continues to change lives three-quarters of a century later. We adopted as our watchword a phrase Sam had coined; we committed ourselves to "making Pittsburgh as famous for God as it is for steel." And we sought ways we could do things together across denominational lines.

Despite seeing abundant blessings on our local ministry, John and I were deeply grieved over the growing drift in the Episcopal Church away from biblical teaching on many issues. Bishops and clergy who denied every tenant of the creeds they had promised to uphold went undisciplined. An almost complete repudiation of the biblical teaching that Christian marriage is between one man and one woman in Christ had begun. And the long slide of diminishing attendance and membership, which continues up to the present moment, was under way.[57] What could we do to strengthen the church and reverse those trends?

We decided to align ourselves with the Evangelical Fellowship in the Anglican Communion (EFAC). Fairly robust in

---

[57] The high-water mark of membership in The Episcopal Church was in 1966 when there were over 3.6 million Episcopalians in the United States. The Office of the General Convention (the governing body of TEC) reported that domestic membership in 2022 had dropped to 1,584,785, with an Average Sunday Attendance of just 372,952.

England and other countries around the globe, EFAC was just getting started here in America, drawing together a handful of like-minded, biblically conservative Episcopalians in scattered parts of the country. We were warmly welcomed when we attended a strategic planning meeting, and – to our surprise – John was elected President, our old friend Peter Moore was elected Vice-President, and I was elected Secretary-Treasurer.

We changed the name of the American branch to the less cumbersome "Fellowship of Witness." And we began holding regional conferences for clergy and laity around the country. We created a quarterly magazine, *Kerygma* (now called *Mission and Ministry*). We sought speakers for the conferences, and writers for the magazine, who presented biblical truth winsomely, and who encouraged Episcopalians to hold solidly scriptural and evangelical positions. I edited the magazine, and John and I both spoke at many of the early conferences. John was fond of saying, "We need to create our own heroes."

And we worked at doing that. Though we were based in a local parish in a suburb of Pittsburgh, we were both beginning to be known in other parts of the country. John Guest was being invited to do evangelistic meetings that introduced Episcopalians – and many others – to Jesus in a personal way. And I was being asked to do teaching weekends for congregations and dioceses. As the triennial General Convention of the Episcopal Church approached in 1973, the Fellowship of Witness joined several other "renewal" movements in TEC to form an umbrella organization that took the name "Pewsaction." The first syllable was an acronym for **P**rayer, **E**vangelism, **W**itness, and **S**ervice.[58] The several member

---

[58] Pewsaction originally included The Anglican Fellowship of Prayer, The Bible Reading Fellowship, The Brotherhood of St. Andrew, The Conference on the Religious Life, The Daughters of the King, the Fellowship of Witness, and The Fisherman. Eventually some twenty-two renewal groups became part of the coalition, which supported conferences and workshops throughout the 1970s and 1980s.

organizations shared a common display area in the exhibition hall at Convention, and jointly sponsored a prayer booth that offered continual intercession for the Convention itself and the larger work of the church.

Albany Bishop Allen Brown commented that the only thing really "working" at the General Convention that year was the Prayer Booth set up by Pewsaction. As we met and worked with other organizations, it became ever more apparent that to change the church we needed to raise up new leadership. And to do that, we needed to offer solid, biblically based theological education unlike what was being offered in the Episcopal seminaries in America. Pewsaction sponsored a series of National Conferences on Renewal that met annually for several years. And at the first of those Conferences, John Guest made the following announcement: "We in the Fellowship of Witness are committed to seeing the establishment of a new theological seminary in the Episcopal Church, one that is thoroughly biblical and evangelical." Thunderous applause exploded from the audience, which rose to a lengthy standing ovation.

John and I traveled to England, hoping to persuade John Stott, long-time rector of All Souls Church in London, to become the seminary's first Dean/President. Stott warmly endorsed the vision, but said he was not the man for that job. Instead, he recommended Bishop Alf Stanway – the Missionary Bishop who had so impressed me eight years earlier. The Bishop had retired from his responsibilities in Tanzania and returned to his native Australia where he had become Deputy Principal of Ridley College, Melbourne. Alf heard the call of God in our invitation, and he and his wife Marjory moved to Sewickley the following year. He set up an office in the small house we were able to purchase for them, just around the corner from where Karen and I were living, next to St. Stephen's Church.

Alf traversed the country, raising money and interest, and he began pulling together a small initial faculty. Astonishingly - in just over a year's time - we held the opening convocation of Trinity School for Ministry in rented facilities in the next town over.[59] There were seventeen students in the first class. Trinity now has over 150 students in residence and over 1.000 graduates serving throughout the country and around the world. Several of its graduates have become bishops in the Anglican Church in North America. At the opening convocation, Bishop Stanway said, "I remember when we were being trained for the compulsive military service we had in Australia. There was a chap next to me who was waving his gun around wildly. The sergeant-major said, 'Man, if you aim at nothing, you're bound to hit it!' So what are you aiming at? Are you like Paul, who said, 'I make it my ambition to please Christ in all things'?" In founding Trinity, our goal was to please Christ. That remains Trinity's goal today.

1975 was a very eventful year for our little family. Just as Trinity was being birthed, our second child was on his way into our lives. There's a lovely backstory to that. Back during our time at Miss Porter's, one of the students had a dream that God would give us another child, and we would name him John. That wouldn't be a surprising choice, but she shared her dream with us as a prophecy. And now it had been six years since Kathy's birth, and no second child. We began wondering whether the prophecy was true. Was there some medical problem? Testing didn't reveal one. Karen set aside a month of intensive prayer, asking God to reveal his will about all this, and at the end of that month she attended a *Women's Aglow* meeting where gifts of the Holy Spirit were in evidence. In addition to the program being presented, prophetic words were shared. She had asked God to speak to her about a baby during that meeting and was in tears that no such word was given. But as

---

[59]TSM was originally called Trinity Episcopal School for Ministry, but in the forty-six years since its founding it has attracted students from both Anglican and other protestant backgrounds. TSM officially severed its relationship to the Episcopal Church in 2022.

everyone was getting up to leave, a woman ran to the microphone. She said, "Ladies, wait! I'm sorry; God gave me a word at the beginning of the meeting, but I was too frightened to give it. Now I'm afraid *not* to give it. He told me to say that someone here has been praying for a baby, and he wants you to know that you *will* have that baby and it will be healthy and whole."

Karen said, "That word is for me!" She came home and said, "We're going to have a baby." "Where in the world have you been?" I asked. She was pregnant within days, and nine months later John Wadsworth Howe III made his appearance.

In the meantime, my father's long battle with Multiple Sclerosis was ending. Dad was hospitalized again, and this time he would not be going home. The doctors worked very hard to save him from the pneumonia that set in, but he never recovered. Instead, he went to be with the Lord on March 4 – just four and a half months before his namesake came into the world. My dad passed away and 4 months later my son was born. And, once again, God had big changes in store for us.

Chapter 6

Truro, A Local Ministry Reaching Out to the World

Each builder must choose with care how to build on the one foundation that has been laid; that foundation is Jesus Christ (1 Corinthians 3:10-11).

I had been at St. Stephen's for about three years when my bishop, Robert Appleyard, asked if he could begin submitting my name to parishes seeking new rectors. I had expected to be with John Guest for at least five years, but if the bishop was making that request, I needed to be open to it. I began to ask myself, and ask the Lord: if I were to become a rector, what would I try to implement? What would I want to accomplish – with his help? Four things emerged as very clear priorities. I wrote them down in the small notebook I always carried:

1. **Work *with* the vestry.** I had seen in far too many churches the hugely negative consequences of the rector making unilateral decisions. When he moves ahead without the strong support of his vestry, even if he is right, he's wrong. In one congregation, the rector called an assistant by casting the deciding vote on a night when two members of the vestry were out of town (and he didn't allow them to cast their votes in absentia). It nearly split the congregation.

    Meanwhile, some congregations - notably St. Paul's Church in Darien, Connecticut, where Terry Fulham was rector – had adopted policies of unanimity. No major decision would be made until *all* the members of the vestry agreed.

Terry asked: "Does God have a will for this church?" [Obviously, yes.] "Can he communicate his will?" [Only if we are listening.] "If a vestry is divided on an issue, what does that tell us?" [Someone isn't listening! Maybe *nobody* is listening; maybe everyone is voting his/her own opinion, rather than seeking the Lord's direction.]

I wondered, could that policy work elsewhere?

2. **Every member ministry.** The New Testament teaches there are no spare parts in the Body of Christ. There are different gifts, different ministries, different forms of service, but every member of the church is called by God to exercise a unique and necessary role.[60] The job of the leaders is to "equip the saints for the work of ministry" (Ephesians 4:12), and it is the job of the "saints" (all the people of God) to discover and develop the gifts God has given them and use those gifts both in the church and in the world.

   Sadly, in too many places the mindset is that "the job of the minister is to minister, and the job of the congregation is to congregate."

   I thought: if I could teach girls at Miss Porter's to lead Bible Studies in their dormitories, surely I can teach adults to do the same in their neighborhoods. I

---

[60]See especially St. Paul's extended metaphor in 1 Corinthians 12 that the Church is like a human body in which each member is dependent on all the others. The two things we must never say are: "*I* am not needed" (verse 15) and "*You* are not needed" (verse 21).

envisioned developing a whole network of Bible-study-based neighborhood small groups.

I was committed to "giving away" as much of the ministry as possible to members of the congregation. I asked, what would it look like if "each and every part is working properly"? (Ephesians 4:16)

3. **Fifty percent outreach.** I envisioned translating the principle of "loving our neighbors as we love ourselves," and "doing unto others as we would have them do unto us" into the financial commitment of giving away half of the parish income.

    Pastors are fond of telling their congregations (especially at stewardship time!) that "you can't outgive God." I asked, what if a congregation were to practice that corporately? What would God do with such a congregation?

4. **Care for all the members.** Would it be possible for the members of a congregation to be so committed to each other that they would shoulder the burdens of each other's illnesses, accidents, bereavements, job losses, family crises, or whatever?

    St. Paul wrote, "If one member suffers, all suffer together; if one member is honored, all rejoice together." (1 Corinthians 12:26)

    I asked myself: what would it look like if that principle were fully realized in a given congregation?

I interviewed with several vestries in the Pittsburgh area, and occasionally with some as far away as Des Moines, but none of them developed into a call.

In 1975 Karen had a dream in which she heard the Lord saying, "Virginia." Shortly after that a fellow named Jim Whittaker telephoned. He said he had heard me speak at one of the Fellowship of Witness conferences, and he wanted to nominate me for rector of Truro Church in Fairfax, Virginia. I didn't know anything about Truro at the time, but I agreed. I soon learned some background.

Truro Parish was created in 1732, named after Truro Church (now Diocese) in Cornwall, England. Initially Truro Parish encompassed all of northern Virginia. The first congregation established in the area was the Falls Church, where George Washington had worshipped and served on the vestry, and several other members of the vestry served at various times in Virginia's House of Burgesses.[61] In 1843, the Falls Church planted a congregation in nearby Fairfax that met first in the courthouse and then in a private home. The first building on its present site was built in 1933, and the church grew steadily until there were more than a thousand members in the early 1970s.

The previous rector, Raymond Davis, had been there for twenty-seven years, and during the last few years of his ministry he had been influenced by the charismatic renewal. He brought in many of the well-known charismatic and Pentecostal teachers of the late sixties and early seventies, including Derek Prince, Graham Pulkingham, Dennis and Rita Bennett, Bob Mumford, Corrie ten Boom, and others.

Their teachings had been warmly received by most of the congregation, and the church was considered a "renewal parish," with a strong emphasis on the work of the Holy Spirit. Parishioners had been encouraged to seek the supernatural gifts of the Spirit, especially speaking in tongues, interpretation, and prophecy. Sadly,

---

[61]For a full account of the colonial beginnings of the church see *The History of Truro Parish in Virginia*, Philip Slaughter, George Jacobs and Company, Philadelphia (1907)

Dr. Davis's health had failed about two years previously, and his young assistant, Steve Noll, fresh out of seminary, had been priest-in-charge since then. Steve had enlisted the help of a group he called "Shepherds" to visit newcomers and shut-ins. Now they were looking for a new rector.

I submitted a resume and answered a set of questions…and then heard nothing for several months. The Search Committee looked over my application, and determined I was too young (age 33) for the position. But they didn't notify me of their decision, and my folder was put aside. They received 146 applications, and as they neared the conclusion of their process someone realized they had never communicated to me that I was no longer under consideration.

They decided they had kept me waiting so long that they owed me a closer look. The whole Search Committee – 21 members – came to Sewickley to meet and interview Karen and me, have dinner together at a nearby restaurant, and attend St. Stephen's on Sunday morning and hear me preach. Their Sunday visit ended up being pretty funny. They wanted to be anonymous, so they decided to split up, sending seven Committee members to each of our three services, and they strategized that coming from different directions to those services no one would notice them.

But in 1976 the Episcopal Church was getting used to a new Prayer Book. And one of the innovations was "passing the peace." Following the General Confession, the celebrant reaffirms God's forgiveness, then says, "The peace of the Lord be always with you." To which the congregation responds, "And also with you." At that point everyone is encouraged to stand and greet the folks nearby by shaking hands or extending a brief hug, signifying that we are "at peace" with each other.

But, at St. Stephen's, we were not doing that. We were simply giving the verbal response: "And also with you." No standing up, no hug or handshake. So…on the morning of their visit, in each of our three services, when I said, "The peace of the Lord be always with you" seven members of the Truro Search Committee jumped to their feet wherever they were in the congregation…and looked around for someone to hug – and then realized they were the only ones standing. They were *definitely* noticed!

Nevertheless, a week later Truro's Senior Warden (Chairman of the vestry) called to say the Search Committee had unanimously recommended to call me as rector, and the 18-member vestry had unanimously affirmed that recommendation. With a mixture of excitement and trepidation, I accepted.

I was to start officially on March first, 1976, but on the weekend of my start date, both John Guest and I were invited to the National Conference on Evangelism in Dallas, Texas, hosted by the Presiding Bishop, John Allin. As we travelled together, I shared with John my anxiety over the responsibilities I was about to take on. His counsel and ministry, and especially his prayers that weekend, were enormous gifts from the Lord, and the conference itself was a great encouragement on the eve of this new beginning. Thank you, John, and thank you John Allin.

Karen and I were given the option of buying our own home – with a housing allowance – or having the rectory renovated. We chose the rectory. It was located next to the church, but had initially been built as a private home a generation before the Civil War. In fact, during the War, that house was used by Union General Edward Stoughton as his headquarters until he and some of his men were captured there one night by "the Grey Ghost," Confederate Colonel John Mosby. The story has it that Mosby got past the guards, ran up the stairs, smacked the sleeping General across his butt with a sword, and asked, "Have you ever heard of Mosby?" To which the General replied, "Yes; have you captured him?" "No; he's captured you!" And in what would become our master bedroom no less!

The house has bullet holes in its back wall, and the soldiers billeted there had covered the walls of a third-story closet with their artwork, signatures, and graffiti (which we were able to move to the Fairfax Museum). It was (and is) a historically important building, but for us it became a lovely and gracious home where we raised our growing family for the next thirteen years. Our youngest, Jessica, was born less than a year after we moved in.

To share Lent with the Truro congregation, I went to Fairfax several weeks before the renovations were finished, leaving Karen, Kathy, and John in Sewickley. I arrived at Truro on Ash Wednesday, and I gave the first of six meditations on the book of Ephesians as a Lenten "get acquainted" series. Six weeks in Lent, six chapters in Ephesians; an easy match. I had no idea the six weeks would turn into thirteen years, and we would cover nearly every book in the Bible.[62]

The small staff I inherited included Steve Noll who, as I mentioned, had been "priest in charge" for the previous two years. Though he was now back to being an Assistant, I hoped he would stay on for the long haul. He joined me in sorting out some complicated pastoral issues – including salvaging a couple of marriages that were in significant trouble. His knowledge of the parish was very helpful. But Steve sensed God's call to the academic life and left for graduate studies during my first year in Fairfax.[63]

Sunday morning worship at Truro was typical of most Episcopal churches, but there was also a Sunday evening service in

---

[62]Most of those lectures have been digitized and they are available without charge at biblebanquet.com.

[63]Steve did his PhD. in Biblical Studies at the University of Manchester, where he studied with F.F. Bruce and Barnabas Lindars. He was for 21 years Professor of Biblical Studies and Academic Dean at Trinity School for Ministry, and then became the first Vice Chancellor (President) of the Uganda Christian University, which grew from 750 to over 10,000 students under his leadership. He has been a major contributor in the theological shaping of the Anglican Church in North America (ACNA) and the Global Anglican Futures Conference (GAFCON).

the Chapel where a small singing group led contemporary music, prayer was spontaneous, and the gifts of the Spirit were often in evidence. This was reminiscent of The Barn, but new to me in an Episcopal setting, and I loved it from the start. My initial impression was that God was wonderfully real to this congregation, but, having had numerous visiting preachers each offering a different theological perspective, a good, solid, consistent Biblical foundation had never been presented. Perhaps that was what God sent me to Fairfax to provide.

I decided to have no guest speakers for at least the first year. I committed to preaching from the lectionary as a discipline. It would force me to deal with "the whole council of God" (Acts 20:27) rather than simply riding my own favorite hobby horses. Parishioners responded enthusiastically as we began to open the scriptures together. The Wednesday evening lectures drew about 200 people. And the Sunday evening services began to grow.

Several times each year we gave an explicit invitation for people to surrender their lives to the Lord, in an initial commitment or in renewing or deepening their relationship with Jesus. Usually, I asked that they come forward and kneel at the communion rail while the rest of the congregation prayed for them. Taking such a visible, public step is often a turning point in someone's life, as it marks a decisive new beginning. I often asked people to join me in using *John Wesley's Covenant*:

"I am no longer my own, but yours. Put me to what you will. Put me to doing, put me to suffering. Let me be employed for you or laid aside for you, exalted for you or brought low for you. Let me be full, let me be empty. Let me have all things, let me have nothing. I freely and whole-heartedly yield all things to your pleasure and disposal.

And now, glorious and blessed God, Father, Son, and Holy Spirit, you are mine and I am yours. So be it; and the covenant now made on earth, let it be ratified in heaven. *Amen*."

But we also tried to instill the realization that *every* time a person comes forward to receive the communion elements it is literally a response to an altar call. When I first got to Truro, the eucharist was celebrated only on the first Sunday of each month. It soon moved to every other week, and ultimately it was clear we wanted to do this every Sunday.

At my first vestry meeting I discussed the unanimity principle. There was great skepticism: "No decisions until *all eighteen* of us agree? No way is that going to happen! We're thirteen miles west of the District of Columbia – *nothing* is decided by unanimity around here!" But then someone commented: "You know, John has just been called with a unanimous vote of both the Search Committee and the vestry." Someone else said, "Well, maybe that could work for the *really important* decisions, but we can't maintain it for everything all the time!"

"Why don't we try it for three months?" I suggested. The vestry agreed. (How much damage can he do in three months?) We quickly learned that unanimity didn't come automatically. We had to work at it. We reminded each other that we were not seeking *grudging acquiescence*; we were looking for *enthusiastic agreement*. That meant anyone having an objection needed to share it with everyone else. And we needed to take all opinions very seriously. In effect, this gave every member of the vestry an absolute veto. Seventeen others could think we should do something, and one vote to the contrary was enough to stop it.

The adoption of unanimity invested each member of the vestry with enormous dignity: "my one vote counts more than seventeen others combined." But the corollary was that people were careful not to exercise such authority casually. Adopting unanimity didn't mean we always came to agreement immediately. It meant that when we were *not* agreed we simply wouldn't decide that issue that night. We might put it off until the next meeting or have a special meeting to consider it more carefully. After the three months had passed, several people who had been on the vestry previously said they had never seen the business side of things move so smoothly. Why? Because we didn't go home winners and losers. We went home all winners. And the further lesson was that when agreement didn't come immediately, we almost always saw later there were reasons why doing what was initially proposed would have been a mistake.

We decided to continue the practice indefinitely. We made a "covenant" with each other that if ever we needed to decide urgently, and we were not agreed, any member of the vestry could call for an ordinary majority vote and we would be bound by it. In the next thirteen years, that happened only once. The first time one of the women in the congregation wanted to pursue ordination, one of the vestry members insisted we take a vote so he could oppose it, based on his belief that women should not be ordained. Interestingly, several years later he told me he knew he was quenching the Spirit when he cast that vote. "The Holy Spirit was telling me, 'Let her minister,' but I couldn't do it." I asked him, "Have you told her?" "Oh yes," he said. And he became one of her strongest supporters.

One night we had an especially urgent question before us. We went around the table, and there were as many different opinions as there were people in the meeting. Someone said, "Let's pray." We did. Then we went around the table again…and there were still as many different opinions as people. (That surprised me, as I thought God would tell everyone I was right! And no doubt all the others thought the same thing about their opinions.) I said, "We didn't do that well, did we? Let's try again. And this time, let's try to put our own ideas away and ask the Lord to speak to us. Maybe he will give someone a scripture. Maybe a vision. Or a word of knowledge."

We prayed again. I saw a vision of the Lord Jesus on the cross. I don't often see visions, but this was very clear. It was like a close-up on a movie screen. And then I saw the Roman spear slam into his body, and I heard the words, "Out of his heart shall flow rivers of living water." I said to everyone, "I have no idea what this vision means. That's a verse out of John, chapter seven, and it has nothing to do with the crucifixion. It was Jesus' own promise about the Holy Spirit being given to those who believe in him." A man across the table said, "I know exactly what it means. God is saying: if we would be those out of whose hearts will flow rivers of living water, we must be those whose hearts are broken by the things that break God's heart." There were several additional words of prophecy. When we voted for the third time, we were unanimous. And the decision was different from anything previously suggested.

I have always tried to honor my predecessors, so I asked the vestry if we could refurbish our meeting room in Raymond Davis's honor, and when they agreed I asked Karen's father to paint a full-sized oil portrait of Dr. Davis to hang there.

I met with the Shepherds and discovered that several of them were interested in beginning the kind of neighborhood groups I hoped to develop. I gave the first of many "Shepherd Group Training Courses," consisting of three major sections:

- **How to lead an inductive Bible Study.** As with the girls at Miss Porter's, the goal was not to become great *teachers*, but to learn how to ask the kind of questions that help people discover the message of the scriptures for themselves.

- **How to share the Gospel**. We need to expect that as people get into the Bible, they will begin to realize that some of the others in the study seem to know God in a way they themselves do not. Whether they can articulate the question or not, they will find their hearts are asking how they too can know God personally. We need to know when that question is being asked, and we need to know how to answer it.

- **How to give rudimentary counseling**. As people study scripture together, they will inevitably also share their personal lives. They will begin to pray with each other. They will share their needs. We need to know how to respond Biblically to such sharing. And we need to know our limits: when do we turn to professional counselors for help?

I was very fortunate to have in the congregation a gifted Christian psychologist, Dr. Jim Osterhaus, to guide us through that third section.[64]

We started with six Shepherd Groups. My goal was to have at least 50 such groups, enough to have one in every neighborhood where we had parishioners. That included folks from Northern Virginia, D.C., and Maryland. We even had people commuting from Fredericksburg, over an hour south of us. I insisted that when a Shepherd Group regularly had more than about a dozen people attending, it should spin off a new group, simply because most homes (and driveways) cannot accommodate many more people than that. Being so close to the nation's capital, the population in Northern Virginia has a turnover rate of about 20% each year, which resulted in many of the Shepherds being transferred to many other places, taking their training with them. In effect, we planted Shepherd Groups around the globe.

---

[64]Dr. Osterhaus is the author of nine books to date, including *Red Zone, Blue Zone: Turning Conflict into Opportunity*, written with Joseph Jurkowski and Todd Hahn.

Splitting off new groups is always the hardest part, as it feels like breaking up friendships. But if we refuse to do this, the original group will soon reach the point of maximum size, and no one new can be added. Dividing is the key to multiplying, and it keeps both the old and the new group fresh.

Two months after going to Truro, I asked Bishop Alf Stanway to lead a one-day retreat for our vestry. He talked about the very different personality types included among Jesus' first apostles, and that just as they needed (and no doubt irritated!) each other, so the many different people on any church board or vestry must find room for opinions, perspectives, and insights different from their own. At the end of the day, we had a leisurely time of prayer. In the middle of it, one of the men said, "I think I'm hearing a word from the Lord. *I believe he is saying he wants us to give away half of our income!*" Another said, "I confirm that." And within moments all eighteen members agreed that was a word from God. I had not mentioned that was one of the four goals I had written in my notebook, but it was a deep confirmation to me that this was on God's agenda for us.

At that point, Truro's outreach budget was 13% of our income – 10% to the Diocese of Virginia, and just 3% to "other." The question was: how do we get from 13% to 50% in a time of double-digit inflation, while we were carrying a large mortgage, our staff was frankly underpaid, and we needed to hire additional staff for our rapidly expanding congregation?

I proposed a "Seven Year Plan": the first year we would take a small step and raise our outreach to a total of 15%. Then, in subsequent years, we would increase it 5% per year. (I don't think anyone realized at first that we were talking about *compound interest*. Five per cent of $1,000 is one thing; five percent of $100,000 is quite another.) But, to our astonishment, when our Stewardship Call came around each year there was an *overage*. The congregation pledged more than the vestry asked. The third year the overage was so great that we jumped from 25% to 40% outreach, and we achieved the goal of 50% outreach in five years, instead of seven.

Each month we began our vestry meeting with a passage of scripture and a brief meditation. Usually I spoke; sometimes it was one of the vestry members. As the third year Stewardship Call was approaching, I gave a brief meditation on the Biblical tithe: ten percent, off the top, before taxes, given to the Lord and the work of his Church. One of the members said, "I have never heard that before! Would you be willing to write that up, and we can all sign it and commend it to the congregation?" There was unanimous agreement. That didn't mean all the vestry members were already tithers – some were not – it meant they committed themselves to getting there and they were willing to urge others to do the same.

I said, "OKAY. But if we are going to call people to tithe, I want us to be clear it is tithing to the Lord, not necessarily tithing to Truro Church." I suggested we invite people to make *unsigned* pledges. "We need to know at least approximately what we expect to receive – so we can make responsible decisions. But we don't need to know who is giving what. Let's let that be between each person and God." So we devised an unusual pledge card. On one side was the actual pledge: "I plan to give so much to the work of God through Truro Church." And we invited people to consider checking either of two statements:

- *I am committed to the Biblical standard of tithing, and this pledge is a portion of that pledge given to the work of God through Truro Church.*

Or:

- *I am committed to the Biblical principle of tithing, and this pledge represents a definite step in a specific plan to get there.*

On the other side of the card, we invited people to write a letter to themselves: "What is the Lord saying to me today, and what am I saying to him?" Tear that side off at the perforation; seal it and address it to yourself. Then, come forward, and place both sides in a huge offering basket in front of the altar. We said: "Nine months from now we will mail the letter back to you, never having read it ourselves, as a reminder of what transpired today." God blessed our approach. That was the year when our overage was so great that we dropped two years from our Seven Year Plan.

Every-member-ministry became increasingly important. For instance, as Truro's numbers increased, I realized I could spend nearly all my time just visiting people in hospitals around the Capitol Beltway. We had parishioners from Virginia, Maryland, and the District of Columbia. Visiting all of those in the hospital at any given moment could constitute a full-time ministry. I offered a six-week course in hospital visitation, and about two dozen people took it. It shared several simple and basic lessons I had picked up: be brief, friendly, optimistic; do *not* say, "You think that's bad? Let me tell you what happened to me!" Do *not* sit on the bed. *Do* ask if you can pray with patients. And respect their wishes if they say no. (Most people will welcome your prayers. If anyone says no, simply pray for him after you leave.)

I said, "Here is your assignment: Take one lunch hour next week and visit the hospital nearest where you work. Check in at the welcome desk and ask to see the list of religious preferences. Visit anyone from Truro, and, for that matter – if you have time – visit any other Episcopalians on the list. And let's report back what happens when we get together next week."

Two or three of the people came back saying, "This is definitely not my ministry!" But most reported wonderfully encouraging visits. And several asked, "Can I do this more than once a week?" We suddenly had a cadre of nearly 20 hospital visitors! Instead of my trying to do it all myself, I had multiplied myself twenty times over, and we had lay people asking for the opportunity to do more! Of course, I still visited the desperately ill and dying, but routine hospital visitation became a lay ministry.

The guiding principle soon became train, equip, and deploy members of the congregation to do the work of ministry. And they did it! There were at least two instances of people's lives literally being saved because, when facing emergencies, they turned to the leaders or other members of their Shepherd Groups. They didn't feel close enough to the clergy to call us, but they trusted the Shepherds in their neighborhoods to help when the need occurred.

Bob Van Houten came to see me one day. He said, "I've taken every course you offer, and I don't seem to fit in any of those ministries. I can't lead a Bible Study. I can't do personal counseling. I'm not very good at sharing my faith… I've been a civilian government worker for years, and I can afford to retire. I just want to do ministry. Is there anything for me?"

"Bob, what do you like to do?" He seemed surprised by the question, but I have discovered that most of the time, if a person likes doing something it's because he or she is good at it. (That's not always true; some folks should confine their singing to the shower!) If they are good at it the question is: how can they use this gift, this talent, to serve God and bless others? After a moment Bob said, "I don't want to brag, but I can do anything with my hands." "What do you mean?" I asked. "I can do anything: carpentry, plumbing, electricity, painting, brick work, whatever…I just wish there were a ministry for me."

I said, "Bob, the physical plant is yours." And Bob spent the next three years going from room to room in all five buildings of our complex, repairing, renovating, rebuilding. Wherever people would see him working it was almost like there was a little electric motor humming. Bob exuded the joy of the Lord as he brought our aging facilities into the best shape they had ever been in. And when he finished the job, he had a whole new career of doing the same thing for parishioners in their homes. If they could pay him – great. If not – it was his gift to them and to the Lord.

I had a similar conversation with Wendy Tierney. "What do you like to do?" "I love to prepare a wonderful meal for people." "How about doing exactly that, once a week? We will invite anyone who wishes to enjoy a good, inexpensive meal to come to Tuesday Luncheon. You cook; we will charge a few dollars, and I will give a brief Biblical meditation." Tuesday Luncheons grew to be a very popular offering in downtown Fairfax, and Wendy soon had a dozen other women working with her every week.

My psychologist friend, Jim Osterhaus, developed the Biblical Counseling Center, anchored by himself and two other professionals and parishioners they trained to assist them.

We took down the walls between three small rooms on the first floor of our education building and developed the Truro Bookstore, making Bibles, good Christian literature, and our own growing tape ministry easily available to parishioners and others.

Truro began to attract other ministries to relocate in Fairfax, and soon we were able to lease the four-story office building across the street, which we renamed the International Christian Ministries Building. It housed Christian Stewardship Ministries, Episcopal

Renewal Ministries, CMJ, (a Christian Ministry to Jewish People), the Institute on Religion and Democracy, Five Talents (seeking to empower the poor in developing countries), and another eight or nine national and international organizations who wanted to share space in a central location.

We had a couple in the congregation named Jerry and Mezzie. Jerry was Jewish, and Mezzie was a charismatic Christian. Each year they invited a group of about forty friends, half Jewish and half Christian, to join them for the celebration of the Passover meal. They stretched tables together from one end of the living room to the other, and Karen and I were invited to join them one year. I found myself seated directly across from Jerry. One of the Bible passages that is always read at the Passover meal is from Psalm 118:

> The stone that the builders rejected has become the
> chief cornerstone. This is the Lord's doing; it is marvelous
> in our eyes (118:22-23).

I asked Jerry, "What do you think that refers to?" He said, "I don't know." I said, "I think it is Jesus." He was silent for a long moment, then said, quietly – but in the hearing of all his guests – "I think you're right." The following Sunday was Easter. I said, "Why don't you come, and receive Jesus at his Table this Sunday?" He did. He was baptized shortly thereafter.

Our time at Truro Church was a very heady time! It seemed that the more our commitment to outreach grew, the more God enabled us to do locally. Newcomers were joining the congregation every week. The Shepherd Groups were steadily growing. People were coming to Christ and being filled with the Holy Spirit. God seemed to be blessing everything. Following a vestry meeting one of the men said, "I have never had so much fun in my life as I'm having on this vestry!"

And having blessed Karen and me with the birth of John during our last year in Sewickley, the Lord surprised us just sixteen months later when Jessica arrived, during my first year at Truro. Our quiver was full.

Joe Kitts, an Englishman who had been in seminary with John Guest, joined our staff as my Assistant Rector. Joe had been a coal miner before hearing God's call to ministry. He was fond of saying he had gone "from the pit to the pulpit." Joe had an amazing gift of evangelism. People would go see him about some personal issue, and moments later they would be on their knees asking Jesus to become their Lord and Savior.

An elderly parishioner named Henry had memorized not only many passages of the King James Bible, but most of the collects in the *Book of Common Prayer*. He could recite them as easily as most people can repeat their favorite song lyrics. But one huge disappointment for Henry was that his brother Arthur didn't know the Lord. He prayed for Arthur every day of his life. Henry died, and Joe Kitts preached at his funeral. And during that funeral, Arthur accepted Jesus.

My second Assistant (after Steve Noll) was Neil Lebhar, whom we had first known at Loomis. Neil was a senior when I first went there as Chaplain. We had wonderful conversations with him, and Karen led him to the Lord at our kitchen table. Following Loomis, Neil did his undergraduate work and the first two years of seminary at Princeton. He then transferred to the Virginia Theological Seminary in Alexandria in 1976, the same year that I began at Truro.

Neil was my first seminarian-in-training, and after ordination he became an Assistant and then my Associate Rector. Neil had a superb ministry with children and young families, and a quirky penchant for telling shaggy-dog jokes and stories. He served with us for many years before accepting a call to Jacksonville, Florida, where he eventually became the first bishop of the Gulf-Atlantic Diocese of the Anglican Church in North America.

The *Life in the Spirit Seminars* we held introduced a growing number of parishioners to – well, life in the Spirit. Our Sunday evening service was growing. We started with about two dozen, meeting in the Chapel, then moved to the undercroft, and finally we had to move into the church itself, as no other space was large enough. We moved the service to Friday nights, and visitors from around the Beltway – Virginia, Maryland, and DC – joined us for what we called our Prayer and Praise service: a combination of wonderful worship songs, testimonies, spontaneous intercessory prayer, a Biblical teaching, and always an informal celebration of the eucharist.

Often there were words of prophecy and speaking or singing in tongues. Frequently there were healings. Sometimes quite dramatic ones, as when a man tore off the brace he was wearing because his twisted leg was suddenly straight. Another time, a goiter the size of an orange shrank to nothing during the week it had been prayed for.

Of course, not everyone we prayed for was healed. A parishioner asked if I would visit the young daughter of some friends in the Fairfax Hospital who was battling leukemia. Lisa was as gentle and sweet a person as I have ever met, and my heart melted in sympathy for her. I prayed with her and her parents, Randy and Sandy, and she went into remission. I visited her at home several times, but the terrible disease returned and soon Lisa was back in hospital. Sandy said their pastor believed Lisa was too young to be baptized, as she wouldn't understand it; so would I be willing to baptize her there in hospital? Absolutely! It was hugely reassuring to all three of them to know Lisa belonged to Jesus when her brief life drew to a close.

One of our men left his wife to embrace a gay lifestyle, and contracted AIDS. He had stopped attending church or meeting with his Shepherd Group, but – despite the near-universal horror and dread everyone had of AIDS in those early days of learning about it – not only I, but several members of his group visited him in hospital, prayed with him, held his hand, and anointed him with oil. He died with reassurance and hope.

The Friday night Prayer and Praise service grew to more than a hundred. Then twice that number. Then it doubled again, and finally usually drew over 500 folk each Friday. We continually said to visitors: "We don't want you to leave your home churches on Sunday mornings, but we are delighted to have you join us on Fridays for Prayer and Praise."

I was being asked to share what God was doing and what he was teaching us at Truro with other churches around the country. I organized some of the things we were learning from the Lord into a conference structure that I shared in many other churches and dioceses around the country. I called it "Seven Principles of Parish Renewal." (Not *the* Seven Principles, as if we had somehow discovered everything that could be said on the subject, but simply seven of the major things God had been showing us.)

- *Discover your gift and major in it.* This applies to all Christians, but I began with the clergy. It is unlikely that God has strongly gifted any of us in all areas of ministry, so – with the help of your parishioners – try to discern what you do best, what God blesses when you do it, and invest in that area especially.

- *Provide for all the other needed ministries.* I had learned from my time with John Guest that he was so strong in evangelism that I needed to balance things by leaning into teaching. If you are "majoring" in one area, bring in others who can balance your ministry in areas where you are not as strong.

- *Equip and deploy "subpastors" in a network of home groups.* This directly reflected our experience with our Shepherd Groups. If the issue is worship and celebration, the more the merrier for worshipping God with a thousand other Christians is an exhilarating experience. But if the issue is belonging, it is a very different matter. We don't *belong* to a thousand others. We *belong* to ten or a dozen people who know and love us deeply, friends with whom we can study, share our lives, and pray with and for each other.

- *Provide for the systematic teaching of scripture as the center of the Christian life.* If teaching is your strong suite, do it yourself. If not, bring in those who can unfold "the whole counsel of God." (Acts 20:27) Don't be content with a twenty-minute sermon once a week. "Faith comes by hearing and hearing by the word of God." (Romans 10:17). If you want a strong congregation, with strong believers in it, give them large portions of good Biblical teaching.

- *Adopt unanimity as the basis for decision-making.* This was easily the most controversial part of the conferences, but when I shared our experience of waiting upon God until he brought us into agreement it made sense, and many other vestries began to "experiment" with it as we had done.

- *Develop a vision for outreach.* I shared our experience of moving to fifty-percent outreach and cautioned people not to be scared by it. We didn't get there immediately, and our first steps were small ones. I told the story of a

"98-pound weakling" who admired a big strapping lumberjack. "Do you know what I'd do if I were built like you? I'd go out into those woods and find me the biggest, meanest, ugliest grizzly bear and I'd rassle him to death!" The lumberjack smiled, and replied, "There are a lot of little bears out in those woods."

- *Pitch worship to the highest degree of excellence possible.* Do whatever you are doing as well as you can possibly do it, whether it is singing the great classical hymns of the church, offering contemporary praise music, or preaching the Gospel. Give the Spirit of God freedom to move in your services. The service leaflet should be the agenda for the meeting, not the minutes. Let God have his way, whether on Sunday morning or in a Prayer and Praise type of celebration at some other time in the week.

Often, I would take a team of parishioners with me. Several folks initially nervous about public speaking found God was opening new venues of teaching and witnessing for them after they shared in one of these visits.

Truro had supported *The 700 Club* from before my time as Rector, and I became friends with both Pat Robertson and his co-host, Ben Kinchlow. Both taught at two of our annual all-parish retreats. I tried to dissuade Pat from running for the presidency of the United States in 1988, but when he determined to do so I hosted a meeting for him with northern Virginia clergy. Pat renounced his ordination vows when he made that run, and when he "reaffirmed" them in a nationally televised *700 Club* event twelve years later, he asked me – by that time a Bishop – to be one of the participating clergy. He said, "The historic Church must be represented." They interviewed me on *The 700 Club*, and Ben asked, "What would you say to others who hear about what God is doing at Truro?" "I would tell them: Come and see for yourself."

I was elected President of the National Organization of Episcopalians for Life (NOEL). Originally founded in 1966 as Episcopalians for Life by Bishop Joseph Harte of Arizona, NOEL produced an occasional newsletter to a small list of supporters. We incorporated in 1983, and began sponsoring regional conferences, publishing a regular quarterly magazine, and lobbying both the church and the government regarding matters of life and death. I met with various governmental officials, including President Ronald Reagan, in the Cabinet Room in 1986, and in 1988 we spearheaded the passage of a General Convention resolution declaring that "All human life is sacred, from its inception until death… While we acknowledge that in this country it is the legal right of every woman to have a medically safe abortion, as Christians we believe strongly that if this right is exercised, it should be used only in extreme situations. We emphatically oppose abortion as a means of birth control, family planning, sex selection, or any reason of mere convenience."[65]

(Sadly, that position held for only three years, until the subsequent General Convention, which reaffirmed TEC's long-standing "pro-choice" stance.)

As the summer of 1988 approached, an event was being planned that would redirect Karen's and my life. Approximately every ten years the Archbishop of Canterbury invites all the active bishops of the Anglican Communion to come together for several

---

[65] Resolution A054 of the 71st General Convention of the Episcopal Church. Note: in 2006 NOEL changed its name to Anglicans for Life as its ministry expanded to the wider Anglican Communion. The Resolution is printed in full in Appendix E.

days of study, prayer, and consultation on matters before the Church and society in what is called the Lambeth Conference.[66] Two of the most prominent leaders of the Renewal Movement in Anglican circles during the Twentieth Century were Terry Fullam, Rector of St. Paul's Episcopal Church in Darien, Connecticut, and Michael Harper, President of the Fountain Trust in England, and a former Associate of John Stott. They proposed that – since the bishops were already planning to come to England in 1978 – why not ask those who were involved in spiritual renewal (in its many expressions) to come early and build a pre-conference conference around them?

Thirty-two bishops, including the then – Archbishop of Cape Town, Bill Burnett, attended the Leaders' portion of the Conference, along with about 250 other clergy and laity, including Karen and me, for an amazing week of worship, study and sharing, culminating in a three-hour long eucharist in Canterbury Cathedral. The final two days were open to the public, and we filled the Cathedral. Donald Coggan, the 101st Archbishop of Canterbury, greeted the Conference and startled everyone with his opening comment that "I pray every day for the death of the Charismatic Movement." (Gasp!) After a short pause, he added, "because God never intended a 'movement.' He intended a *Church*, full of his Spirit." The Cathedral exploded in

---

[66]The first such Conference was held in 1867, and until 1968 the Conferences were held at Lambeth Palace, the London home of the Archbishop of Canterbury, located across the River Thames from the British Houses of Parliament. Retaining the name, the "Lambeth Conferences" are now held every 10 years at the University of Kent, overlooking Canterbury Cathedral. The Anglican Communion is a world-wide network of forty-one autonomous provinces, each with its own primate and governing structure. It constitutes the third largest denominational constituency in Christendom, after the Roman Catholic and Orthodox Churches. The Anglican Communion is currently a "house divided against itself" over matters of doctrine and ethics. Due to deep theological disagreements, followed by the Covid pandemic, the Lambeth Conference did not meet between 2008 and 2022, when approximately 650 bishops attended. The Episcopal Church, USA, is officially part of the Anglican Communion, although many of the other provinces consider themselves to be in "impaired" or "broken" communion with TEC. The Anglican Church in North America is recognized by most, but not all, of the other provinces, but it is not officially recognized by the Archbishop of Canterbury.

applause! The Spirit of God was mightily evident during our days together.

In addition to spending over half of our time in worship, with an emphasis on listening to God, we broke into nine working groups that addressed the topics of worship, community, revival and renewal, parish renewal, evangelism, social action, ministry and leadership, spiritual gifts and healing, and ecumenism. Our concern was not what *we* had to say on these many subjects, but what we believed *the Lord* was saying to us about them.[67]

The closing eucharist was especially dramatic. Just before the service began, I found myself sitting next to a man fondly nicknamed "Mr. Pentecost." David du Plessis was a South African Pentecostal minister, one of the key figures in the early days of the Renewal Movement in the main-line churches. Du Plessis had been a young associate of an even earlier leader with the funny name of Smith Wigglesworth. It is said that Wigglesworth had every recorded miracle of Jesus replicated in his ministry, including raising the dead! In the few minutes we had to speak together before the service began, Du Plessis told me of an extraordinary encounter he had with Wigglesworth when he was a young man. He said, "In 1936, Smith Wigglesworth was staying in my home, and one day he burst into my study and told me he had just had a vision from the Lord. He said that God was calling me to bring the message of the Holy Spirit's power to the great churches of Christendom. He said, 'David, I will not live to see it, but you will see some of the great cathedrals of the world filled with people praising God with speaking in tongues and in the power of the Spirit.'" He continued, "I saw the first fulfillment of that prophecy at the great Charismatic Congress in Rome in 1975, and I am seeing it again in this Conference tonight."

---

[67]The reports of the Conference were published in a slim booklet called *A New Canterbury Tale*, with an introduction by Michael Harper; it is still available from Alibris.

In addition to a stirring sermon by Bishop Festo Kivengere (of Kigesi, Uganda), who often is called "the Billy Graham of Africa", there were several prophecies given, including one that correctly predicted that some in attendance that evening would face martyrdom for their faith. A woman from Colorado just "happened" to visit the Cathedral during the service, only to find herself sitting next to Bill Frey, the Episcopal Bishop of Colorado. She asked him, "What is that strange ritual up there where people are falling down as others lay their hands on them?" He told her that sometimes when people are touched by the Holy Spirit, it so overwhelms them that they cannot stand. (This is sometimes called "swooning" or being "slain" in the Spirit.) And he gently led her to put her trust in Jesus.

One prophecy went on for several minutes. It said the stones surrounding us in the Cathedral were witnesses crying out to us of what God had done in ages past, "But this I say to thee – that I have greater things to make than this great building. I have a *living* work to do with stones that live in infinite and gracious detail in the quarry of my heart..." It was in a kind of blank verse, and it sounded like a cross between Isaiah and Shakespeare as it rang out across that ancient Cathedral and held us spellbound. The prophecy was caught on audio tape and is included with the reports of the Conference in *A New Canterbury Tale*, and I have reproduced it in Appendix D of this book.

The man who gave the prophecy was a British banker named James Haig-Ferguson, and – astonishingly – in ordinary conversation he stuttered so severely that he could hardly speak a sentence. About ten years later, I happened to meet him again, and I asked him about it. I said I have read that sometimes people with a severe stutter find they can sing or recite poetry, even though ordinary speech is difficult for them. "Is that why you prophesy the way you do, almost in poetry?" "No," he said, "if I *tried* to do that it would only make me more tongue-tied." Suddenly I realized he was speaking almost normally, and I asked him about it. He said, "As I have been faithful in exercising the gift of prophecy over these past few years, God has been healing my stutter."

Back at the Cathedral, at that closing eucharist, the thirty-two bishops sat in a great semi-circle behind the high altar, and Archbishop Burnett was the celebrant. It was a powerful reminder of the twenty-four elders seated around the throne in heaven that we read about in the book of Revelation. The music included both the ancient hymnody of the Church accompanied by the mighty organ of Canterbury Cathedral and contemporary praise music led by the Fisherfolk from the Community of Celebration.

After the Archbishop gave the benediction, the Fisherfolk broke into a final song: "I will sing, I will sing a song unto the Lord…" and a moment later thirty-two bishops had joined hands with each other, and they were *dancing around the high altar*. I was horrified! These are *bishops,* and this is *Canterbury*!

And immediately I was rebuked in my spirit. If the Lord Jesus were to walk into this Cathedral tonight, do you think we would all sit on our hands? We'd be shouting and clapping, and dancing for joy. And he *is* here, filling this service, and filling his people with his Holy Spirit.

The Conference was designed as a stand-alone event, but it gave birth to a new kind of missionary agency called Sharing of Ministries Abroad, initially led by Michael Harper in England, and now with parallel sister agencies in a dozen other countries around the globe. (It also goes by the acronym SOMA, which is also the Greek word for "body.")

At the invitation of a local bishop, SOMA sends teams of clergy and lay volunteers on ten-to-fifteen-day mission trips to "share" their ministries – whether they are ministries of evangelism, teaching, healing, developing spiritual gifts, establishing a prophetic community, addressing issues of marriage and family, discovering anointed worship, etc. The volunteers pay their own expenses, and to the extent possible the churches in the diocese being visited provide accommodation for the team while they are there. SOMA has sent such teams to about fifty countries to date, many of them deeply impoverished. Karen and I have participated in these and similar ventures in about twenty countries.[68] We have seen such efforts change not only the churches, but regions and countries.

On our first SOMA visit we stayed with Bishop Sundar Clarke and his wife, Clara, of the Diocese of Madras in South India. We visited several of his congregations, most of them in very poor rural communities, and we were struck by the generous hospitality they invariably showed us. No matter how much or how little they had, they were gracious to share their best with us. It was a joy to us to see the way God was using Sundar and Clara to bring Hindus to faith in Jesus.

From there we traveled with Bishop Sundar to Singapore for a gathering of about forty international leaders. The Bishop was carrying a huge burden concerning division in the Church over the changing role of women, and when he shared that with us, I thought, "We should wash his feet." Before I could mention it, another delegate made the same suggestion. In western circles foot-washing seems like an odd ceremony rooted in a very different culture, but in Indian villages it is still a common courtesy to offer it to visitors who have walked dusty paths, just as it was in Jesus' day in ancient Palestine. To Bishop Sundar, it was gesture of compassion, and tears of gratitude ran down his face.

While in Bombay (now called Mumbai) we also visited some Hindu friends of my sister Linda. They gave us an extravagant vegetarian luncheon in their second-floor dining room. As we were

---

[68]In all we have been privileged to visit 62 countries on six continents, and all but five of the fifty states in the USA.

finishing eating, a man who had been on the balcony all along without our realizing it, leaped in through the window. He was dressed in rags, and our hosts told us he was a "holy man" staying with them to discern the propitious timing for their daughter's wedding. He patted me gently on my chest and arms, and said, "You are saint of God...I, too, am saint of God." Then he reached somewhere inside his rags and pulled out a small vial of mercury. He poured it into his palm and gently massaged the liquid until suddenly it was a small marble in his hand. No, that isn't possible! But this was his "proof" he was a "saint of God." We concluded that India is a land full of magic, superstition and even demonic powers.

Terrible drought ravaged South India in the mid-1980s, and we discovered that digging one well for about one thousand American dollars could literally save a village. Over the next few years, a partnership developed between Truro Church in Fairfax, Virginia and the Diocese of South India and we provided funding for about one hundred such wells. Of course, the majority of villagers in most places were Hindu, and when they asked, "Why are you doing this?" the answer was "Because God loves you, and he proved it by sending his Son to die for you." Many Hindus accepted Jesus and were baptized in the water drawn from these wells.

Sundar and Clara visited Truro annually, and our parishioners loved to hear both of them in the pulpit. (Several remarked, "He's a great preacher, but she's even better!") When the Bishop said, "I do not ask you for Cadillac automobiles, I do not ask you for fancy television sets; I ask you for a cup of cold water in Jesus' name," people dove for their wallets. We had groups of parishioners in Fairfax praying for Indian Christians in Madras and Indians in Madras praying for Truro members in Fairfax.

Two years after India and Singapore, I was asked to do the morning Bible Studies for a SOMA gathering in Fiji. Delegates came from Aotearoa, New Zealand, and Polynesia. Bishop Jabez

Bryce greeted us with the comment, "I have one of the largest dioceses in the world. Of course, over 90% of it is wind and waves."

We met for a week, and I focused on the seven churches in Asia Minor to whom the letters from Jesus in Revelation 2 and 3 are addressed. My theme was that in each city the Church struggled with both history and ethos – as does every church in every locale in all of history. The question is always, "Will we be agents of change, or chameleons of culture?"[69] St. Paul wrote, "Do not be *con*formed to this world, but be *trans*formed by the renewing of your minds."[70] Or, as J.B. Phillips renders it in his paraphrase, "Don't let the world squeeze you into its own mold."

Fiji is a spectacular tourist destination for those who can afford the five-star-hotel life. But this was not a conference for the wealthy. The delegates were housed in YMCA facilities where we slept on straw mattresses and had no running hot water. The bedroom walls didn't reach all the way to the ceilings – in order to permit air flow, as there was no air conditioning. One startling dimension of being there with so many charismatics was hearing several of them speaking in tongues as they slept!

These SOMA conferences were chaired by Michael Harper. Leaders came from many different parts of the world, and after months of planning and prayer, when we finally came together Michael always began with the question, "Now, why are we here?" Everyone had a general sense of what God wanted to accomplish, but we couldn't see it completely until God fitted together the bits and pieces of hopes and dreams, prayers and possibilities, personalities, and spiritual gifts, like the pieces of a jigsaw puzzle.

---

[69]Much of this teaching is on the *Bible Banquet* recordings in the series Revelation Part 1.
[70]Romans 12:2

Whenever Karen and I did one of these mission trips we asked members of our congregation to stay with our children. On one trip to Australia that responsibility fell to my Assistant Rector, Bill Reardon and his wife Marilyn. Bill had been the Archdeacon of the diocese of Southern Virginia before joining the Truro staff. Bill and Marilyn met us at the airport when we returned. "I need to tell you, there was an accident," he said. "John [age 8] jumped from the swing-set and broke his arm. Don't worry; he is doing fine."

But then, as we moved to the baggage collection area, Bill amended his report: "Actually, he broke both arms. But he really is doing fine." (Bill thought we would handle the news better if we received it in two parts!) Happily, it was true that John was doing well, and he recovered from his fall without any long-term consequences. We were so grateful for the several couples who supported us by caring for our kids while we were being "sent from God" to other parts of the world.

Karen and I had the amazing privilege of visiting the Holy Land three times during our Truro years, twice with Terry Fullam, and once with Pat Robertson. All three times we enjoyed remarkable experiences of the Lord. On our first trip we brought about forty parishioners with us, and on our day in Jerusalem the crowds were especially large. We were hurried through each of the sacred sites. When we got to the Upper Room[71] we had only enough time to take hands together in a large circle and give thanks to God for what he did there so long ago. But, as we did so, one of our men was struck by the Holy Spirit and he suddenly began speaking in tongues. No one had asked God for that to happen; no one had prayed for it. Gifts of the Holy Spirit were not on anyone's mind at that moment. But the man was literally ecstatic, and his wife jumped back from our circle as if she had received an electric shock.

---

[71] Probably not the actual Upper Room of Jesus' time, but approximately where it had to have been located.

On our second visit, Karen and I became separated as we made our way through the shopping area in the ancient Roman Cardo. Somehow that triggered in her a deeply rooted anxiety that neither of us had previously realized she had. She became deeply distraught at the thought I had abandoned her, and even after we found each other about an hour later, she still couldn't shake it off, and spent hours in tears. Our friends, Al and Lois Brickner, who were by then living in Jerusalem, said that in their experience "Jerusalem is like a spiritual pressure cooker" – things that might take months or years to unfold elsewhere might be revealed in days or hours there. We prayed with them, and God graciously released Karen from an insecurity she had not known she carried.

There were three amazing highlights of our third trip to the Holy Land, this time with a large contingent of fans and supporters of *The 700 Club*. We began this third visit with a leisurely boat ride across the Sea of Galilee and a worship service on the boat which ended up a healing service. One man, wounded in the Korean War and unable to bend his back ever since then, was wonderfully set free of all pain and paralysis. He happily kept reaching down and touching his toes for the rest of the trip.

Second, we participated as a group in "Jerusalem 2000," a great celebration that brought thousands of believers from all over the world together to praise God in the Valley of Hinnom, the very place where centuries previously children were offered as living sacrifices to Molech and other Canaanite deities. It was a glorious preview of that day when "at the name of Jesus every knee will bend in heaven and on earth and under the earth, and every tongue confess that Jesus Christ is Lord, to the glory of God the Father." (Philippians 2:10-11)

And third, we again visited the Upper Room. This time, we had the place to ourselves. Terry Meeuwsen, one of the co-hosts of *The 700 Club,* said she wanted to sing for us. She offered a beautiful

Israeli melody praising Jesus, and as she hit the final note a white dove flew directly over her head. I asked Pat Robertson, "How in the world did you arrange *that*?"

Going to Truro meant seeing God at work in many different places, bringing people to himself all over the globe, and it has been one of the great privileges of my life. It also involved meeting a young priest from Tanzania named Gerard M'Pango. His Archbishop, The Most Reverend Musa Kahurananga,[72] recognized his leadership potential, and sent him to the Virginia Theological Seminary in Alexandria for further education and training. Gerard found his way to Truro and began worshipping with us. In addition to his tribal language, Gerard spoke Swahili and was fluent in English. He had an engaging personality and a wonderful sense of humor, and he quickly became a very welcome part of our congregation. About halfway through his time at VTS he got a letter from the Archbishop saying that he had been elected Assistant Bishop of his diocese. He hadn't known he was even under consideration!

But there was an important stipulation: "You must find a wife and get married before coming home." (African Bishops and Archbishops have a good deal more authority than do their American counterparts.) Gerard somehow found Margaret, a young lady from Tanzania, living with her brother, a businessman, in Washington, DC. Gerard and Margaret dated for several months, and when he asked her to marry him, she said Yes. The Archbishop said he would travel from Tanzania and join me in officiating at the wedding. Our congregation was delighted to see all this happening in our midst, and someone suggested we give the young couple a

---

[72] "Musa" is Swahili for "Moses," and it literally means "saved from the water." Musa Kahurananga was a first-generation Christian. He and his whole family converted from their tribal religion to Christ when they heard the gospel shared by Anglican missionaries. Musa said, "We knew from my grandmother that above the many gods we worshiped there was the one true creator God. We just didn't know he had a Son."

bridal shower. That was not a custom Gerard and Margaret were familiar with, and when they arrived at the home of Neil and Marcia Lebhar where the party was held, they seemed extremely nervous.

The party was lovely, and Gerard and Margaret received more presents than they knew what to do with. But as the afternoon wore on and the time came for people to begin leaving, Gerard asked Neil, "Is that all there is?"

"Gerard, people have been incredibly generous!" Neil responded. "How can you ask if that's all there is?" To which Gerard whispered: "But aren't you going to *wash us*?" (After all, isn't it called a wedding *shower*? Strange American custom!)

One serious wedding issue did arise. Margaret needed a wedding dress, and they didn't have money to buy one. Then one of our church secretaries said, "You know, there is a dress in the sacristy. It's been there for years, and I have no idea who left it. Why don't you see if it is something you can use?" Everyone trooped in to see and applauded when it fit Margaret as if it had been made for her. It was beautiful and needed zero alterations!

In spite of these blessings, on the morning of the wedding the bride got cold feet! When he heard that Margaret was backing out, the dismayed Archbishop said: "I will speak with this young woman." I have no idea what he said, but it was effective, and the wedding went on as planned. Our daughter Jessica, and the Lebhars' daughter, Katie, were flower girls, and the church was packed and jubilant.

Gerard invited Karen and me to come to Tanzania for his consecration as Bishop, and he asked me to preach on that great occasion. We flew to the International Airport in Kilimanjaro and spent the night nearby in Arusha, having our own little Prayer and Praise service in our hotel that evening. Gerard had arranged for the

Missionary Aviation Fellowship to fly the four of us across country the next day. We drove across town to the much smaller local airport and waited next to the dirt runway for the single-engine, five-seat plane to arrive. We hoped we could squeeze all four of us, our luggage, and the M'Pangos' wedding presents into the plane.

Finally, the Cessna 208 broke through the cloud cover, and the pilot taxied up beside us. He climbed out, and his first words were, "Oh, they didn't tell you?" (Don't you love conversations that begin that way?)

"Tell us what?" I asked.

"There's no gas in Mwanza," he said.

"OKAY – um, what does that mean?"

"This plane can only fly about halfway across the country before it needs to refuel. And there is no gas in Mwanza, so I will have to carry gas with me. I'm afraid one of you will have to stay here."

We were horrified, and Gerard immediately took charge. "I'll stay," he said.

"Gerard, how did you decide that?" I asked.

"I'm not going to leave my wife here, and I can't leave either of you. I'll stay."

I shook my head. "Gerard, you're the only one of us who absolutely has to be there!"

Turning to the pilot, I said, "There's only one fact here: we're not splitting up. Isn't there someplace else we could go for gas?"

"Well," he said thoughtfully, "there might be gas in Tabora. It's on the way."

"Why don't we go there and see?" I asked. "At least we'll be half-way there."

"OK, but you're going to have to leave your luggage."

I shook my head. "Do you remember what Moses said to Pharaoh?" I asked.

"Moses said 'We will go with our flocks and our herds…*and not one hoof shall be left behind.*'" (Exodus 10:9 and 26)

"But," the pilot argued, "We'll never get off the ground!"

I said, "Let's try."

So we crammed ourselves in, with luggage and presents in the cargo hold and piled on our laps, up to the ceiling. We must have looked like the Beverly Hillbillies on an airplane! It shuddered and shook as the pilot used every inch of runway, and it lifted off…just barely…clearing…the…trees…and we made our way to Tabora… where – yes – there was gas.

Gerard was about to become the Assistant Bishop of Western Tanganyika working directly under Archbishop Kahurananga. A brand-new Cathedral was under construction when we arrived at the diocesan compound in Kasulu. The builders were determined to have it sufficiently completed in time for Gerard's consecration two weeks later. Gerard had arranged for Karen and me to tour the diocese, meet as many of the clergy as possible, and do some teaching in each of the villages we visited. Even today most of the Anglican clergy in Tanzania have only a rudimentary Biblical education, and he asked me to help him lay a stronger theological foundation as his new ministry was about to begin.

I had not planned to focus on the theme of healing, but I quickly discovered that was a subject of great interest everywhere we went. Tanzania is a poor country, and, except in the major metropolitan areas of Dodoma and Dar es Salaam, there are relatively few doctors and hospitals. And a great many sick people. The Anglican Church in Tanzania was planted by British evangelicals who taught that miracles, signs and wonders, and healings were given by God to authenticate the preaching of the Gospel during the first century after Christ. They believed that with a few rare, wonderful exceptions, these miracles no longer occurred. When I told them that at Truro we were seeing God do frequent, amazing healings in answer to prayer – everyone wanted to hear more about it.

"Do you think he would do that here?" they asked.

"Why don't we ask him?" I replied.

And so began an astonishing series of meetings across the Diocese of Western Tanganyika in which we witnessed miracles at every stop. After the first meeting the word spread, and scores of needy people began showing up. I urged the clergy who came to the meetings to join me in praying for the sick. It seemed that the Lord didn't care who was doing the praying; he was answering us all.

In mid-week, someone said, "If you really believe God can heal anybody, please go pray with the Archdeacon; he is very ill."[73] So I sought him out.

"Archdeacon, what's the matter? Would you like me to pray for you?" He opened his mouth, and showed me ulcers in his mouth and throat, that he said went all the way down to his stomach. "But," he said, "I don't believe in that healing stuff!"

"I didn't ask if you believe in it; I asked if you'd like me to pray for you."

"Well, if you have to," he said reluctantly.

So I prayed for him. It seemed to make no difference. He said he would be going to the nation's capital, Dar es Salaam, for medical treatment that weekend, and he would miss the consecration.

But the day of the day of the consecration, there he was. "Archdeacon," I said, "how are you doing?" He opened his mouth, and the ulcers had disappeared! "But," he said, "I still don't believe it!"

On the evening before the consecration, I sat with Gerard in a diocesan Land Rover, overlooking the compound, and I said, "Gerard, you know you are not going to be able to do this ministry without the help of the Holy Spirit." "I know that," he replied. "Let's ask him to fill and anoint you for everything that lies ahead." He agreed, and I prayed for him, and then I told him, "I think God wants to give you the gift of tongues. Just like on the Day of Pentecost. Praise him as the Spirit gives you utterance – just not in English or Swahili!" Gerard had never spoken in tongues before

---

[73] An Archdeacon is usually a Deacon, sometimes a priest, who has been asked by the Bishop to take on significant oversight of a group of other Deacons or a particular area of ministry in the Bishop's diocese.

(and he never did so again). But that evening, he opened his mouth and for the next 20 minutes the most beautiful cascade of praises to God in a language neither of us knew or understood poured from him, as the vehicle shook mightily.

Let me jump ahead for just a moment to an email I received from him over three decades later, on the day after Pentecost in 2011. He was visiting the US, and he wrote in part:

> "Yesterday I went to worship at Christ the King Church here in San Diego, California. Because it was Pentecost Sunday, when I was given time to greet the church, I took the opportunity to share my spiritual experience on the day before my consecration 30 years ago. Do you remember that, John? Do you remember how I shook that car during the infilling of the Holy Spirit and the speaking in tongues? That was the most edifying spiritual experience in my life. All my gifts of leadership, etc., took off from there.
>
> "That is why I was able to grow my diocese up to 500 congregations and over half a million members by God's grace. After working for 20 years, we had to elect three more assistant bishops to assist me. By the time I took early retirement last year, the diocese had already been divided into three more dioceses of Tabora, Shinyanga, and Sumbawanga. That has all happened because of your prayer that afternoon, Saturday before my consecration. So, thank you very much, my brother, for what you did that day for me. When I shared this the congregation erupted into a thunder of applause. Praise the Lord."[74]

    Actually, I did nothing but pray; the Holy Spirit did it all!

---

[74] I shared this excerpt in a previous book, *Anointed by the Spirit*, Creation House, 2012, p. 119. It is from a personal email sent to me by Bishop Gerard M'Pango on June 13, 2011, and he gave me permission to include it.

Gerard's consecration was a lavish spectacle, combining Anglican liturgy with native African singing, drums, and dance, and the Cathedral was packed, with people sitting in the window openings where the glass had not yet been installed, and standing around outside. I tried out the few Swahili phrases I had learned, "*Jambo!*" (Hello.) "*Jina Langu ni* John." (My name is John.) "*Asante sana.*" (Thank you very much – for having me here.) Then, I continued with the help of a translator.

During the offertory people brought gifts of money, clothing, food (including live chickens), and household items, whatever they could afford, to help the new Bishop and his bride begin their new marriage and his new ministry. And after the service there was a raucous celebration featuring a precious treat they had been collecting for weeks: cases and cases of Coca-Cola. None of it was refrigerated, of course, but it was a rare treat for most of the attendees.

Two surprises were still to come. First, Archbishop Kahurananga made the gracious pronouncement that he was "creating me an Honorary Canon" of St. Andrew's Cathedral in Kasulu.[75] Obviously, this was for the support we all gave to Gerard and Margaret through his time at Truro and their courtship among us. It was an honor I was deeply grateful to receive on behalf of the parish. And second, as the Consecration Service and Reception drew to a close, a young assistant pastor approached me. He said his name was Joseph, and his infant daughter needed healing from God. Would I come to his nearby village and pray for her? "Of course." I replied.

---

[75] A Bishop or an Archbishop will sometimes appoint a "Canon" to an administrative post in a Cathedral or Diocese. An Honorary Canon usually holds no specific Cathedral responsibilities, but a Bishop or an Archbishop will occasionally bestow that title on a lay person or member of the clergy who has performed extraordinary service to the Diocese. (In a play on words, it is often said that a canon - note: one "n" - is a "big gun" in a Diocese.)

We rode with Joseph and two of his friends in a Land Rover to a small village. About a dozen small mud huts with thatched roofs encircled a clearing with chickens roaming around. Several of the villagers stood outside, interested to see what was happening. Joseph's wife brought a beautiful baby girl outside to us and placed her in my arms. "Her name is Christine."

"What's wrong with her?" I asked. "Her tongue is tied, and her womanhood is broken." (I don't know what they meant by that, but I think she had some kind of genital malformation.) I began singing "Jesus loves me, this I know, for the Bible tells me so. Little ones to him belong, they are weak, but he is strong. Yes, Jesus loves me; Yes, Jesus loves me; Yes, Jesus loves me; the Bible tells me so."

Joseph and his wife, their friends, and Karen and I sang together, with tears streaming down our faces – and the neighbors watching. Then I prayed, asking God to "touch and heal her of both of these problems, in Jesus' name. Amen."

There was no visible change, but as we made our way back to Virginia the next week, I couldn't get Christine out of my mind. I wrote to Joseph. "If we could get her to Dar es Salaam, both of those problems could be treated with today's medical technology. May I send you the money to make that happen?" My letter crossed in the mail with one from Joseph. He said that "in the days following our visit, *both of Christine's problems disappeared entirely*! THANKS BE TO GOD!" (Some twenty-five years later, I received a follow-up letter from Joseph, with pictures of his grown-up daughter, still well, and now married with a child of her own.)

As I have reported in this book, Karen and I have seen remarkable healings here in the United States from time to time. But the incidence of healings and other miracles in so-called third-world countries has been much greater and more dramatic. I do not understand this, but I imagine two possibilities about it.

First, we in the Western world rely so much more on science and technology that we are slow to believe God can or will intervene directly in our lives. Whatever we may call it, this is unbelief. Scripture says that when Jesus returned to his hometown of Nazareth, "he could do no mighty works there, because of their unbelief." (Matthew 13:58) On the other hand, when simple believers hear for the first time that God is still in the miracle business, they often leap to a position of such faith that, in effect, they hear Jesus saying (as he did so often during his time among us), "Go in peace, your faith has made you well." (Mark 5:34) And they are healed.

Second, in the closing verses of Mark's Gospel, healings and miracles are promised to those who "*Go* into all the world and proclaim the good news." (Mark 16:15)[76] God promises that signs and wonders will accompany and authenticate the missionary proclaim the good news." (Mark 16:15)[77] God promises that signs and wonders will accompany and authenticate the missionary outreach of Jesus' followers, but they are somehow especially tied to *going.* Wherever we *went,* we saw the healing power of the Spirit at work.

---

[76]Many scholars have questioned whether the so-called "longer ending" of Marks' Gospel (16:9-20) was part of the original manuscript or added later, perhaps in the second century, "by someone who thought the text needed a better ending, especially in light of the promises about a resurrection appearance in Galilee in Mark 14:28 and 16:7" (John R. Donahue and Daniel J. Harrington, Sacra Pagina, vol. 2, The Liturgical Press, p. 463) Whether the text was original or added, the whole history of Christian missions testifies to the frequent appearance of healings and miracles accompanying the initial proclamation of the Gospel to a given people group.

[77]Many scholars have questioned whether the so-called "longer ending" of Marks' Gospel (16:9-20) was part of the original manuscript or added later, perhaps in the second century, "by someone who thought the text needed a better ending, especially in light of the promises about a resurrection appearance in Galilee in Mark 14:28 and 16:7" (John R. Donahue and Daniel J. Harrington, Sacra Pagina, vol. 2, The Liturgical Press, p. 463) Whether the text was original or added, the whole history of Christian missions testifies to the frequent appearance of healings and miracles accompanying the initial proclamation of the Gospel to a given people group.

There was an ironic postscript to our visit. We were scheduled to return to Nairobi for our trip back to the United States, and we had to travel first to Bujumbura, Burundi, to catch our connecting flight. As our wedding anniversary was that week, I had planned an overnight at the famous Treetops Safari Lodge in the Aberdare National Park, just outside of Nairobi, overlooking one of Kenya's most famous wildlife watering holes, before returning home.[78]

But when we reached Bujumbura, we discovered our plane had already left, and there wouldn't be another until the next day. Anticipating that possibility, our friends in Kasulu had arranged accommodations for us at the Christian Missionary Alliance compound. But "accommodations" turned out to be rooms with sheets for walls! Karen asked, "What about malaria?" Our host, Clyde, replied, "Oh, it's not so bad; I've had it three times myself."

I said, "Clyde, I really don't want to be an ugly American, but this is our anniversary, and we were supposed to be at Treetops tonight; this just won't do. Surely, there must be a hotel in town." "Oh, yes, but it is *very* expensive," he said. "That's okay; could you take us there?" He did, to a beautiful four-star hotel on the shore of Lake Tanganyika – and *that's* where we got food poisoning!

Several years later, I did get to visit Treetops with my son, John, but I've always been sorry that Karen missed it!

---

[78] It was during her visit to Treetops in 1952 that Elizabeth II "went up a tree a princess and came down a Queen," when her father, King George VI, died on the night of her visit.

Chapter 7

Expand the Tent

You will spread out to the right and to the left (Isaiah 54:3).

Invitations to share what God was doing at Truro were coming with increasing frequency. The vestry deliberated how we should respond to them, and finally offered me a new contract saying they considered it part of Truro's calling and ministry to encourage congregations and dioceses throughout the country and around the world to experience the outpouring of God's Spirit. And it stipulated that I could be free to accept teaching missions that would take me away from home up to about 40% of my time. (In fact, I did about half that.)

At the same time, our own congregation continued growing. On Sunday mornings we had three full-to-overflowing services, and our Friday evening Prayer and Praise averaged 500 - 600, about half of whom were visitors from other churches. We began to suspect God wanted us to expand our facilities. We consulted several architectural firms that specialized in church buildings, and we quickly concluded that the only realistic way to expand was by adding "lateral transepts" – seating areas on either side of our central worship space with gradually elevated pews facing each other. This would also create additional classroom space in the undercroft area beneath them. They also recommended moving our choir and organ from the loft at the rear of the building and placing them behind the altar at the very front of the sanctuary. If effect, we would be worshipping "in the round" in the style of ancient basilicas.

But this was a hugely daunting prospect! As soon as we began discussing it some parishioners said it was too expensive, too disrupting. We shouldn't even *think* of spending that much money "on ourselves" when we could be sending it to missions and outreach. And anyway, Jesus would probably return before we were even finished with our renovations.

In October of 1981 we began using a special congregational prayer asking God to guide us as we finalized plans for our program and budget in 1982 and as we tried to look beyond the immediate and discover where God wanted to take us. As we approached the November vestry meeting, the vestry and staff agreed to spend a day in prayer and fasting asking God to speak to us with unmistakable clarity, and we invited the congregation to join us in doing that. The question was very simple: *to build or not to build? Does God want us to do this?*

We could see many reasons both for and against, but we didn't want to decide based on *argument*. We wanted God to *speak* to us. For five years we had been making our decisions by unanimity. We realized that doesn't *guarantee* that we are hearing God, but it is surely a restraint against hasty error. And we had learned that when we are truly seeking his guidance, he can bring us to agreement. If we do not agree, we do not proceed. I knew from previous discussions that at least a quarter, perhaps a third, of the vestry were initially opposed to moving forward. So, if when we gathered for our meeting, we unanimously concluded God was saying "Build," it would be a very strong indication of his direction.

When we came together for that all-important meeting, we reminded ourselves of George Mueller's famous dictum: *"If you want to hear the Lord on any given subject, get yourself to the place where you have no vested interest in the outcome."*[79] We asked God

---

[79]Mueller lived in England during most of the nineteenth century. He was a founding member of the Plymouth Brethren, and along with his wife, Mary, he founded and maintained a number of orphanages. He famously trusted God and God alone for his and the children's needs, sometimes sitting down to a meal

to help us let go of our own opinions and seek only his direction. Several members led our prayers for the next ten or fifteen minutes. Suddenly, one of the men who had been adamantly opposed to building, said, "I believe I have just gotten a word from the Lord!" He read from Isaiah:

> "Enlarge the site of your tent and let the curtains of your habitations be stretched out; do not hold back; lengthen your cords and strengthen your stakes. *For you will spread out to the right and to the left*, and your descendants will possess the nations and will settle the desolate towns." (Isaiah 54:2-3; the words I have italicized were particularly striking.)

A vestry member on the opposite side of the table began to weep. When he regained his composure he said, "I was praying in the parking lot before the meeting, and the Lord led me to that very passage. And I asked him, 'If that really is from you, Lord, will you please give it to someone else during the meeting?'" Another member said excitedly, "Look at the promise in verse 3 – '*your descendants will possess the nations*' – it isn't a question of expanding OR doing outreach; it's a matter of expanding *in order to do more* outreach. A bigger church means more people, more giving, and more money for outreach." In another moment, all eighteen members of the vestry agreed: we had heard the Lord.

And suddenly it all made sense: what is the greatest thing we have to offer our neighbors in and around Fairfax? The *discovery of new life in Christ* and fellowship with his people, the *prayer and support* of our rapidly expanding network of Shepherd Groups, *worship* in the Body of Christ as we gather together, the *proclamation of the Word of God*, the *changing of lives*, and the *equipping of people for ministry*. If we can accommodate more people in what God is doing among us, the result of "enlarging the

---

when there were no provisions available, giving thanks to God for what they were about to receive, and suddenly having someone show up with food enough for all.

tent" will be greater resources, more ministry, and many more teams of people going *out*! Expanding in Fairfax will mean increased impact elsewhere.

We had asked our people to join us in seeking God's guidance. I kept a record of the notes I was given by parishioners. The following are a few of the comments I received, in the order I received them.

- Tom and Theresa Mulligan, told me that the day after I asked for congregational prayer support, they received a letter from an Israeli Christian pastor friend living in England. This is what it said: "Greetings in the name of Jesus. Just this morning my eyes fell on the words of Haggai the prophet. It was like the Lord drew my attention to this portion of scripture. 'Is it a time for you yourselves to dwell in your paneled houses, while the Lord's house lies neglected? Now therefore, thus says the Lord of hosts: Consider how you have fared... Go up to the hills and bring wood and build the house, that I may take pleasure in it and that I may appear in my glory... And the Lord stirred up the spirit of all the people, and they came and worked on the house of the Lord of hosts, their God...' I don't know exactly what it is for, but I have to obey the Spirit's prompting. It may have to do with your church, so please discern and ask the Lord. Your servant, Maurice Rubin."

- Dan Williamson said, "The Lord seems to be pointing me to this scripture: 'Whether it was two days, or a month, or a longer time, when the cloud continued over the tabernacle, abiding there, the people of Israel remained in camp and did not set out; but when it was taken up, they set out. At the command of the Lord they encamped, and at the command of the Lord they set out; they kept the charge of the Lord, at the command of the Lord by Moses.' (Numbers 9:22-23) *God seems to be saying it's time to move.*"

- Joyce Hile (a member of our staff) wrote: "With all of you, I have been praying about God's will in regard to enlarging our physical facilities…especially that we might be like Joshua and Caleb who saw what needed to be done immediately rather than wandering around it for years.

  Today it was my turn to read the scripture at Morning Prayer, and I asked the Lord to confirm what I was hearing by having something in the reading that would speak to the subject of building or moving forward. At first glance it did not seem to do this, but then verse 46 from 1 Corinthians 15 jumped out and has continued to stay with me all morning. 'It is not the spiritual, which is first, but the physical, and then the spiritual.' I think he is saying *tend to the physical; go forward, then he will use it for the spiritual.*"

- Carol Deitz: "When I read your letter in November, I felt a profound witness to the construction of lateral transepts and the expansion of the physical plant. A part of that witness was that the Body should be together to hear God's Word."

- From a lady who was not a member of the church, who had simply stopped by to pray: "As I knelt down, I had a vision of the sanctuary stretching on endlessly. I realized that it wasn't the sanctuary itself that stretched out, but the ministry." She said she didn't know any consideration was being given to enlarging the facilities, but she sensed she should share her vision with us.

- Jane McVicker also had a vision of Jesus himself approaching the altar, which seemed to expand as he came near. And she heard him say, "Turn none away from my Table." She said she sensed "strong guidance to make room

- for all those the Lord is and will be calling to his Table here by increasing the facilities."

- <u>On the day of our vestry meeting, a parishioner called to say</u>: "As I was praying, my Bible fell open to Isaiah 49:16-20. "Behold, I have graven you on the palms of my hands; your walls are continually before me. Your builders outstrip your destroyers... Lift up your eyes round about and see; they all gather, they come to you... Surely now you will be too narrow for your inhabitants..."

- <u>Just before the meeting, another person shared from the *New International Version*</u>: "This is what the Lord says, 'Heaven is my throne, and the earth is my footstool. Where is the house you will build for me? Where will my resting place be? Has not my hand made all these things, and so they came into being?' declares the Lord." (Isaiah 66:1-2)

God had spoken, and we were determined to obey him. We asked Bruce Scott, a well-known builder in Fairfax and a member of the congregation to take on the project. He said he could do it, but we would have to vacate the building for several months while the renovations were under way. I said, "We don't want to vacate for a single Friday night or Sunday morning." He said that won't be possible!

But then (while taking a shower!) he had an inspiration. If we would hang heavy plastic curtains (like shower curtains) on the inside of the walls, his crew could work adding the transepts during the week, then clean up on Friday afternoons, and drop the curtains for services during the weekends. It was a bit of extra effort every Friday, but we did it. We didn't miss a service.

But there was another issue. We had to match the bricks that were used in constructing the original church a quarter century earlier. But they were larger and a darker red than anyone was using in the US in 1981. And we needed 40,000 of them! Bruce consulted with every brick supply company on the east coast. Finally, one company in New England said they did have some oversized bricks left from a previous order. "But I don't think you will want them. They were left in the kilns too long, and they are a deeper red than is currently being used."

How many did they have? "About 40,000 of them." They were an exact match.

About half-way through the Church Expansion Project, we realized what no one had anticipated from the blueprints: the girders holding up the roof would have to remain in place and become columns between the original worship space and the new transepts. But, depending on the sight lines, a line of columns can be as opaque as a solid wall. And, for approximately 40% of the new seats we were adding, *neither the pulpit nor the lectern would be visible*!

We had an emergency vestry meeting *in* the church. We looked at the problem from every possible angle. Someone suggested creating a three-tiered central platform like the ones often found in colonial churches: the Lord's Table on the floor level, a lectern raised above it, and the pulpit still higher at the top. But, under that plan, for every seat that would gain visibility from one side, another would lose it from the other. Someone else suggested we televise the services and hang a monitor on the inside of each column. Those in the transepts could see on the screens what they couldn't see directly. Right. In a Georgian colonial church building.

As we left one of the vestry members said to me, "I just know the Lord has some simple solution for us." And I (the spiritual leader of the congregation) in great despair, responded "Not this time." (Oh, ye of little faith!)

But God did have an enormously simple solution! Gordon Kloster, our Jr. Warden, was having lunch in one of the half-finished transepts the next week, and he pondered again the scripture God had given us: "...*you will spread out to the right and to the left*...." He thought, "What if we move the pulpit *to the right* and the lectern *to the left,* placing them directly in line with the columns on their respective sides of the church? It would be like someone standing in a doorway between two rooms. People on both sides would have an unobstructed view." It was a wonderfully simple solution indeed.

But then there was another problem. According to the blueprints for the original building, one of the girders supporting the roof was imbedded in the wall in exactly the place the pulpit would need to occupy. Someone suggested, "Well, we don't *know* it's there. Why don't we dig into the wall and see what's actually in it?" We did. And to our complete bewilderment, we found no girder where the blueprints said there was supposed to be one. Why didn't the original builders follow the original blueprints? We never did figure that out. But evidently God knew we would need the space a quarter century later. We moved the pulpit. And the lectern. And everyone on both sides had an unobstructed view. We finished the project without missing a Sunday. And without having to borrow any financing.

But the Lord wanted us to expand in another way as well. My Assistant, Bill Reardon, came to me and said, "I think I have one last Hurrah in me. I'd like to plant a new congregation in Herndon, the next town west of Fairfax." He asked if I would support him doing that. I said, "Why don't you begin a weekly Bible Study and prayer time for those who might be interested in such a venture, and see if God will raise up a new congregation?" He did so, beginning with about 15 parishioners from Herndon. By nine months later (an interesting gestation period!) there were just over 200 of our people ready to begin.

Additionally, there were those who said they didn't want to leave Truro permanently, but they would help get a new mission launched by attending for the first few months. And a third group said they were not called to be part of the launch, but they would support it with their prayers and giving.

Bill found meeting space in the Franklin Intermediate School, just down the road from his own home, and in late January we called all 200 people forward, prayed over them, and sent them off to begin the Church of the Epiphany.

I was reminded of Bishop Stanway's "Alforism": "Unless you are willing to give away your best, God cannot bless you." We wanted to give away our best, and we also wanted God's blessing. And within about six months, God had replaced the 200 who left. Our plan was to subsidize this new venture at whatever level was required, but as it turned out, the new congregation was self-sufficient from day one. A year later Epiphany was granted full parish status by the Diocese of Virginia, and they broke ground for their first building three months later. I preached at the first service in the new building.

Clearly "Expanding the Tent" had *not* been a choice between building and outreach. We expanded to *enable* outreach. And God gave us his blessing.

In March, 1982, I received a telephone call from a very excited Paul Walter, President of the South American Missionary Society. He said, "Something wonderful has just happened to Adrian Caceres, the Bishop of Central Ecuador. He has had a life-changing experience of the Holy Spirit, and he is looking for someone who can visit Quito and teach his priests about the Spirit's work." He said, "This is one of the most important doors that has ever opened in Latin America. Are you available to go?"

We asked the vestry to pray about this with us, and we all concluded that yes, Karen and I should go. We flew to Guayaquil, where Bishop Caceres greeted us at the airport. He said he had instructed all the clergy of the diocese to come for a week of meetings beginning on Saturday and including Sunday morning (they had arranged for lay people to lead the services in the churches).

The Bishop also said, "You will be my slave; I will kill you!" He meant it as a joke, a way of saying he would make me work hard, but it nearly came true. He also said we should be forewarned: "They may not be completely receptive at first; they had a bad experience with another visiting American. They don't really want to be here." (Not a very encouraging way to begin.)

As it turned out, "all the clergy" from Central Ecuador were eleven priests plus the Bishop and a translator. Most of the clergy had multiple congregations, since the Anglican churches were very small. We were to meet from April 30 to May 7, and being on the Equator, it is always very warm. All but one of them, a priest named George,[80] were dressed in shirt sleeves. For whatever reason, George wore a long black cassock all week. We sat at tables arranged in a square, with Bishop Caceres seated directly behind George, with his back against the wall. Some of the priests spoke a little English, and I had a smattering of high school Spanish. But the translator was very good, and so, following introductions, we began.

I framed the discussion by saying *if you belong to Jesus, you have the Holy Spirit*. St. Paul wrote, "No one can say 'Jesus is Lord' except by the Holy Spirit." (1 Corinthians 12:3) Obviously, he didn't mean no one can *say the words*. I knew a Hollywood actor who more than once played the part of a priest. He could say the *words*, but I happen to know he didn't believe them. Paul meant that no one

---

[80]Pronounced, "Hor-gay"

could say, as an honest expression of his/her personal conviction, "Jesus is my Lord," without having the Holy Spirit.

The question is: *does the Holy Spirit have us*? And the honest answer for most Christians is that we have roped off certain parts of our lives. We have said (in effect), "You can come thus far in my life, but no farther." And the Holy Spirit always wants to go farther – until he has *all* of us. I recounted some of the things Karen and I had seen at Truro and in our travels: the healing of broken bodies and broken relationships, the miracle-working power of God in a multi-cultural church in Singapore, the bishops dancing around the high altar in Canterbury Cathedral, extraordinary healings in Tanzania.

I reminded the priests that St. Peter said we are to "serve one another with whatever gift each of you has received." (1 Peter 4:10) This implies that *every Christian has at least one gift from God*. Our job is to discover, develop, and use whatever gift(s) God has given us, and ask God to equip us with whatever additional gift(s) we might need for whatever ministry he entrusts to us.

Speaking in tongues, prophesying, doing miracles and healings are wonderful, dramatic evidence of the Holy Spirit, but they are not the "be-all and end-all" of Christian ministry. The question is: what is needed in each situation? Having a supernatural gift of healing, for instance, is of no use whatsoever if someone's need is financial. What is needed is someone with a gift of generosity - along with prudence and wisdom in money-management.

I told them about Bob Van Houten and Wendy Tierney, who both exercised their very practical gifts in serving others. But God may want to give us supernatural gifts as well. And speaking in tongues, in particular, opens another channel of communication with God. St. Paul says he will pray "with his mind" (that is, in his own language, which he understands) *and* he will pray "with the spirit" (that is, in tongues, which his mind does not understand unless there is interpretation).[81] I recounted what God had done for Gerard M'Pango on the evening before his consecration.

Bishop Caceres was adamant: he wanted the Holy Spirit, but he did *not* want to speak in tongues!

After the Sunday morning session George approached me. He spoke English well enough that I could understand his question. "What about visions?" he asked. "What about them?" I countered. "I think I just had one! And I've never had a religious experience before," he declared. "So," I asked, "tell me what happened."

He said, "I saw myself in a crowd of people surrounding Jesus just before he ascended into heaven. And I knew I had to get to him. I pushed my way through the crowd, and when I got to him, he turned and asked me, 'Why are you wearing black? You should be wearing white!'" That was it. He asked me, "Do you think it was a real vision? From God?" I said, "I'm sure it was real. But maybe he was speaking about something in your *attitude*, and not literally talking about your *clothing*. Why don't you ask him to show you what it means over the next couple of days?"

That afternoon, about 150 people attended a service that was open to the public. I recounted God's promise to pour out his Spirit on all those who belong to Jesus.[82] I said, "Let's ask him to do that right now. We did. And the Spirit fell. People came forward to receive Jesus. Some began to speak in tongues. Visible healings began. I asked the clergy to join me in praying for others. More people came forward. More healings took place. The clergy were astonished to see God answering their prayers as more and more came forward to receive from God.

---

[81] 1 Corinthians 14:14-15
[82] Joel 2:28-29, and referenced by Peter on the Day of Pentecost, Acts 2:16 ff.

On Monday we debriefed. "This was the greatest day of my life," said one of the priests. Another said, "the high point of my ministry." One said, "I abandoned my ministry four years ago; this restored it." The Bishop said, "The people have more faith than I have. I have wasted so many years."

It had been our own small version of Pentecost.

On Tuesday the topic was: how does the Holy Spirit speak to us today? I suggested that he speaks in many ways: the scriptures (mainly), our conscience, circumstances, sermons, books, other people, and sometimes through visions. I asked George if he would be willing to share the vision he had two days before. He shared with the group what he had told me.

One of the other men asked, "What do you think it means?" I said, "That's between George and the Lord." But George said, "No; I know what it means, and I think God wants me share it." He turned and knelt before Bishop Caceres, and said, "I have hated you. Will you forgive me?" The Bishop could not have expected that, but he responded exactly as he should have: "Of course, I forgive you. Will you forgive me?"

And suddenly a spiritual dam burst. One after another the priests got up from their chairs, crossed the room and spoke quietly to each other, asking forgiveness for ways in which they had offended each other, and for the grudges they held because of those offences. How could there be so many broken relationships in so small a group of men? Especially among men who should have been each other's strongest allies and supporters! It was a good 45 minutes before we could continue. And, of course, after that we had to share the eucharist. It was a glorious, impromptu celebration.

On Wednesday the Holy Spirit gave tongues, visions, singing in the Spirit, and prophecies. Not everyone spoke, but everyone was touched. The two who came into tongues most fully were Bishop Caceres (!) and our translator. He got nouns, verbs, adjectives, adverbs, pronouns. He seemed to have swallowed a whole dictionary! The Bishop said, "What we need in Latin America are charismatic churches! If not, let's pack up and go home. The U.S. is sending a great deal of money down to us. For what? To *conserve*. But we don't need to *conserve*; we need to be a *revolutionary* church." On Thursday we talked about the priesthood of all believers, and that the gifts of the Holy Spirit are for all of God's people for ministry.

Karen and I were scheduled to fly back to Virginia the next day, in time for Truro's annual all-parish retreat at our diocesan conference center called Shrinemont. It was to be an especially important weekend as I had persuaded Pat Robertson to be our speaker. Many people were eager to meet him personally.

But following the wrap-up that afternoon, when I got back to my room I *exploded* with chills, fever, shaking, nausea, and dehydration. We called an emergency physician, who said it was amoebic dysentery, and he said I shouldn't leave the country. By morning I was afraid I *wasn't* going to die. After a week of God doing wonderful healings for so many others, I was the sickest I have ever been. But I said, "No matter what happens, I want to get back home." I called Truro and said I hoped to get there, but somebody else would have to welcome Pat and host the retreat. Somehow I made it to the airport the next day. I couldn't walk by myself, but the flight crew got me into my seat. Just before the plane closed its doors a group of clergy from the conference arrived with a note from all of them. It said simply, "We are praying for you."

And somehow, between Guayaquil and Miami, I was healed. By the time we landed, I was fine. We had a wonderful weekend with Pat who talked the next morning on *The 700 Club* about our Truro people dancing in the Spirit in "a conga line" of jubilation.

And seven years later, Bishop Adrian Caceres was one of the co-consecrators when I became a Bishop.

Chapter 8

Come Up Higher

The Holy Spirit said, 'Set apart for me Barnabas and Saul for the work to which I have called them.' Then after fasting and praying they laid their hands on them and sent them off (Acts 13:2-3).

As far as I was concerned, life in the mid-1980s was just about perfect. I had a beautiful, gracious wife who was teaching part-time at the Christian school our children attended. We had three wonderful, healthy kids who were all doing well academically. The church was bursting with vitality and joy. The huge renovation had been successfully completed without going into debt. We were giving away more than half of our income. I had a daily radio program that was drawing thousands of listeners. The Truro Tape Ministry was producing about 40,000 audio cassette recordings of sermons and teachings each year, and they were being heard throughout the English-speaking world. I was doing numerous parish and diocesan teaching conferences at home and abroad. Karen and I made frequent SOMA missions, and at one point we even smuggled Bibles into communist China. In 1987 I became the President of the National Organization of Episcopalians for Life (NOEL), working to change the church's position on abortion.[83]

---

[83] The Episcopal Church at its General Convention in 1967 expressed its "unequivocal opposition" to any legislation that would "abridge or deny the right of individuals to reach informed decisions" regarding the "termination of pregnancy" or to have an abortion. That stance was reaffirmed in several subsequent General Conventions. The Supreme Court's decision in *Roe v. Wade* was made in 1973. I thought it was one of the Court's most egregious decisions, and I began working with a broad spectrum of others to change both it and the Episcopal Church's stance on abortion. I was the principal mover of the 1988 General Convention Resolution on the sanctity of life which I have included as Appendix E. Sadly, the more "pro-life" position remained in place for only three years.

and, as I mentioned, I was privileged to meet with President Ronald Reagan in the Cabinet Room the following year.

And, having lived for years in church rectories, Karen and I were finally able to find another get-away home like the one we had in New Hampshire. This one was at Lake of the Woods in Locust Grove, Virginia – about sixty miles south of Fairfax. We were able to buy it furnished, and it even came with a boat. I frequently took the Truro staff on overnight retreats at our "lake house." And it was great to share it often with a small group of Northern Virginia clergy.[84] (Back then it only took about an hour to drive to Locust Grove from Fairfax. Today's traffic makes the trip at least twice as long.)

Lake of the Woods had a multi-denominational church that met in the Clubhouse, and they asked me to preach whenever we were there on a weekend and during our summer vacation each year. (Little did I imagine that one day I would become its Senior Pastor.) *Which Way?* was still circulating among young people, and my second book, *Our Anglican Heritage* was being well-received in the Episcopal Church.[85] Our eldest, Kathy, was in an accelerated program that meant effectively skipping two grades. Son John was old enough to begin accompanying me on international mission

---

[84] The four other clergy who usually accompanied me were the Rev. Alden M. Hathaway, Rector of St. Christopher's, Springfield, who became the sixth Bishop of Pittsburgh in 1983; the Rev. David C. Jones, Rector of Good Shepherd, Burke, who became the Suffragan Bishop of Virginia in 1995, the Rev. Henry L. ("Renny") Scott, Rector of the Church of the Apostles, Fairfax, who headed up rebuilding the Atlanta Stockade, a 103-year-old debtors prison into 67 furnished efficiency and family apartments for the urban poor – designated by President George H.W. Bush as one of the "thousand points of light"; and the Rev. John Yates, a much-published author and long-time Rector of the Falls Church Episcopal, Falls Church – who had previously served with me in St. Stephen's, Sewickley, PA.

[85] The first edition of *Our Anglican Heritage* was published in 1977 by the David C. Cook Company. A second edition, co-authored with Samuel C. Pascoe, was published by Cascade in 2010.

trips. And Jessica was becoming proficient in song and dance. We seemed to have found our niche!

But deep disagreements were beginning to surface in the Episcopal Church. Two things transpired at the 1985 General Convention that seemed to foreshadow its eventual breaking apart.

First, the genial but liberal-leaning Edmond Lee Browning was elected TEC's 24th Presiding Bishop. Even before his installation in the National Cathedral in Washington. he declared that under his leadership there would be "no outcasts" in the Episcopal Church. He meant that to be all-inclusive, but most people understood he was announcing his commitment to push for greater openness to gay and lesbian people. He was in favor of same-sex marriages and marital blessings, and the ordination of openly non-celibate homosexual persons. A group of his fellow bishops met privately with him warning that such innovations would split the Church.

They were right, but it wasn't an immediate split. There were many small, and a few very big, fractures over the next two decades and the formation of the Anglican Church in North America in 2009. (More about that later.) Ed Browning was also on the board of Planned Parenthood, which put us on the opposite sides of one of the major issues of the day. I met with Bishop Browning at Washington's National Cathedral five days before he was installed as Presiding Bishop, on January 16, 1986. In spite of our significantly different theological perspectives, I said if he could ever include it in his schedule, we would love to have him visit Truro. Nearly three years later he called to say he could come on December 11, 1988.

As it turned out, that was the day after I was elected Bishop Coadjutor in the Diocese of Central Florida! Ed said that never happened to him before or afterward, and he was up most of the night, rewriting his sermon to acknowledge my new calling.

Second, during that same 1985 meeting of the General Convention, about forty of the conservative bishops began *The Irenaeus Fellowship*, named after the second-century Greek bishop who largely defined Christian orthodoxy in his fight against gnosticism.[86] The Irenaeus Fellowship believed it was time for the various "renewal" organizations in TEC to come together and mount a joint effort to impact both the Church and the larger society. They issued invitations to a four-day conference at All Saints Church in Winter Park, Florida in January 1986. They called it *The Three Rs Conference* – the *Revelation* of God, the *Renewal* of the Church, and the *Reformation* of society. I was invited to attend. The four principal speakers included Peter Moore, who had become Chairman of the Board of Trinity School for Ministry, Philip Turner, Professor of Christian Ethics at the General Seminary in New York, and two British scholars - in some ways representing the "high" and "low" expressions of the liturgical spectrum - the evangelical Anglican professor J.I. Packer, and the Anglo-Catholic Bishop Michael Marshall. It was a rich presentation. Moore asserted the primacy of scripture, Turner set forth the mandate for public witness, Packer stressed the need for unity, and Marshall pictured the Church as a sign of the Gospel.

I was asked to be on a panel of clergy serving in very different circumstances, all of whom were experiencing God's blessings on our ministry.[87] Ninety Episcopal bishops, clergy, and lay leaders from across the country, and from nearly every

---

[86] Irenaeus was the student/disciple of Polycarp, who had known the apostle John, so he was just two generations removed from the first followers of Jesus. He is best known for his book *Against Heresies*.
[87] The others were Keith Ackerman, rector of St. Mary's in Charleroi, PA, who became Bishop of the Diocese of Quincy from 1994 until his retirement in 2008, Carol Anderson, rector of All Angels Church in New York City, and John Guest, of St. Stephen's, Sewickley. All but Carol are now part of the Anglican Church in North America.

organization seeking renewal, converged on Winter Park for this unprecedented conference.[88] The goal of *Three Rs* was to issue a "blueprint" for working together in renewing the Episcopal Church in the last decade and a half of the Twentieth Century. The Joint Statement produced at the end of the Conference explicitly committed these participating organizations to *moving forward together* in revitalizing the Church:

> "Our experience of the presence and power of our Lord in this conference, showing us his truth and pouring out upon us his Spirit within our converging frames of renewal, has led us to resolve that for the future we will pursue renewal within the Episcopal Church, not separately, but together. We shall seek to recover everywhere the realities of love for Christ our Savior, and a simple, childlike obedience to his commands, with which renewal begins."[89]

Emceeing the Conference was my friend, Bishop Alden Hathaway. He had been the Rector of St. Christopher's Episcopal Church in nearby Springfield, Virginia from 1971 until he was elected Bishop of Pittsburgh a decade later. He was one of the clergies who shared frequent overnights at our getaway house in Lake of the Woods. Alden had helped in the founding of Trinity School for Ministry, and he was deeply supportive of the ministry of NOEL. I had not seen him since his move to Pittsburgh. Alden shared with us his perceptions of the special role of a bishop in setting a tone for his/her diocese with evangelical preaching, making church planting a priority, and encouraging parishioners to pursue a personal relationship with Jesus. I was delighted by the way God

---

[88]In some ways the Conference was similar to the International Conference on Spiritual Renewal held in England in 1978, but this was different in at least two ways. First, it was focused on the Episcopal Church, USA whereas the previous one was international. And second, the pre-Lambeth conference was almost entirely charismatic, while this one deliberately incorporated the "three streams" of catholic, evangelical, and charismatic renewal.
[89]Ibid., 147

was using him, both in my own former diocese of Pittsburgh and increasingly on a national platform.

As he was speaking, I suddenly heard another voice, which I recognized immediately. It was the one I heard as I knelt by my bed and gave my life to Jesus as a teen-ager. I heard it again in the little church at UConn. when God told me to go pray with Stu. I heard it a third time when I relinquished my relationship with Karen and the Lord gave her back to me.

The Lord said to me with unmistakable clarity: "*I want you to be a Bishop.*"

I was shocked. "Me, a Bishop? You've GOT to be kidding!" The thought had never occurred to me. I hadn't ever wanted to go into parish ministry, let alone oversee a diocese. I left the conference early and headed home to process it.

Over the next few months, I accepted nominations in three very different diocesan elections: the Diocese of New Hampshire, the diocese that had ordained me – though I had never actually served there; the Diocese of San Joaquin in California – one of TEC's most "conservative" dioceses; and the Diocese of Detroit – one of our most "liberal" ones. As the ordination process unfolded in each of those three dioceses, it became clear that none was really a "fit." But a little over two years after the *Three Rs Conference* I was nominated a fourth time in Central Florida. The diocesan profile looked like it had been written for me. Central Florida wanted evangelism, Biblical teaching, the gifts of the Holy Spirit. There had been a season of renewal on Bishop Bill Folwell's watch, and the diocese said they wanted more of it.

Still, the prospect seemed daunting. Becoming a Bishop is a huge honor, but it is also extremely demanding. It means being in a different congregation nearly every Sunday. Sometimes a Bishop will take spouse and family to a visitation, but much more often the Bishop goes alone. There is an enormous difference between being with the same members of a local congregation week after week - not only for years, but sometimes for generations – and being with a different group of people every week.

Karen then had a strange dream. In it she came home to find our home in ruins, while I was trying to hang a picture on a small part of the wall that was still standing. She called to me, "Don't fiddle with that – we need to get up higher where we can see the extent of the damage." So we made our way through the rubble up to a roof-top balcony, where several people we knew were sitting in rocking chairs – all of them from friends from Florida! She took this to mean that things were beginning to crumble at the local level, but God was calling us (me) "up higher" (to the episcopacy) where I might be able to be of greater influence…and it would be in Florida. After that dream she was sure I would be elected; I was not so certain.

A friend of ours, Mary Ailes, also had a dream she shared with us. She said that in it I was being honored in some very large venue with beautiful paintings on the walls, and an escalator was carrying people from one level to another. She said it seemed to have something to do with a church service, but she couldn't figure out what and it looked like no church she had ever seen.

Still, I wavered. Count the cost. Are you sure you want to do this? No, I'm not at all sure! But I think God wants me to. But is it to be in Central Florida? Maybe. But I don't know if I'm ready. I was in a terrible approach/avoidance conflict. I withdrew my name, thinking that would resolve things. It didn't. I called my bishop, Peter Lee, who advised me to put my name back in, which I did, just a couple of days before the election.

And finally the day of the election arrived. It was held in Orlando. Episcopal elections go on until someone has a majority of votes from both the clergy and the laity. I'm sure my election was prolonged by my having withdrawn and reentered. Our whole family sat by the telephone, as a friend in Florida reported the results of each of the ballots. And, as I received more votes on each of them, I became more confident that this was really what God wanted. And sure enough, on the 13th ballot I was elected Bishop Coadjutor of the Diocese of Central Florida.[90] To our surprise, an hour later our friend Fr. John Yates, who had apparently been following the election as well, knocked on the door and presented me with my first purple bishop's shirt.

Our daughter Kathy had been married at Truro a couple of years prior to the election. The Truro congregation was so much an extended family to us that we invited everyone to attend the service, and we had a double reception following it. Everyone joined us for the first one in the undercroft, then family and close friends went to the second in a nearby restaurant. If leaving Truro would be difficult, leaving Kathy would be much harder.

Now I was being called to serve a much larger and more spread-out family in Central Florida. No church building in the diocese could hold the three thousand people who wanted to attend the consecration service, so we arranged to have it at one of

---

[90]In the Episcopal Church there are five kinds or categories of bishops. The *Bishop Diocesan* is the chief pastor and overseer of his/her diocese. The *Bishop Coadjutor* is the next-in-line, elected to succeed the Bishop Diocesan – usually within about a year, although in some cases it has been a much longer wait. A *Bishop Suffragan* is an associate bishop who does not have a right to succession. An *Assistant Bishop* is a person who was elected somewhere else, now asked by a Bishop Diocesan, with the consent of his/her diocesan convention, to come assist in specific ways. An *Assisting Bishop* is one who serves only occasionally, say to do an occasional pastoral visitation or ordination on behalf of the Bishop Diocesan. I was consecrated Bishop Coadjutor on April 15, 1989, and became Bishop Diocesan on January 1, 1990, the day after Bishop Bill Folwell retired. I served until my successor, Gregory O. Brewer, was consecrated on March 24, 2012.

Orlando's megachurches, Calvary Assembly, with over thirty bishops coming to join in the laying-on-of-hands. We had two choirs, one composed of singers from around the diocese, the other from Truro. When our friend Mary Ailes arrived for the service she said excitedly, "This is the exact building I saw in my dream!" There were beautiful paintings everywhere, and – yes – an escalator taking people from one floor to the next.

Bishop Peter Lee preached the sermon, in it asking me to consider: "What will you do with your hands? What will you do here in Florida as God pours out his Spirit and once again brings signs and wonders for all?" he asked.

Several New Testament passages outline the rigorous qualifications for becoming a bishop,[91] and nearly all the bishops I have known would be quick to admit that every one of us falls far short of God's expectations for us. But, with his grace, mercy, and forgiveness, we press on to "apprehend that for which we have been apprehended." (Philippians 3:12, King James Version).

Shortly after my consecration in Florida, Martyn Minns was elected my successor back at Truro. He invited me to preach at his installation. I began by saying, "This feels a little like preaching at the second wedding of my first wife!"[92]

I inherited a wonderful diocese of 81 parishes and missions,[93] and I hoped to grow that to at least a full 100 congregations by the time I stepped down from office. As it turned out, we were able to

---

[91] See especially 2 Timothy 3:1-7, Titus 1:5-9, and 1 Peter 5:1-4.
[92] Martyn served as Rector until 2006, when he was consecrated Missionary Bishop of the Convocation of Anglicans in North America by Archbishop Peter Akinola of Nigeria. Martyn led a coalition of 11 congregations, including Truro, out of the Diocese of Virginia. He later served as the Interim Bishop of the Anglican Diocese of Pittsburgh.
[93] A parish is self-supporting, and a mission congregation is partially subsidized by its diocese.

"plant" eleven new congregations that survived. (Nationally the survival rate for new congregations is only about 50%). And we were instrumental in helping eleven other congregations become established outside the diocese. (More about that later.) Technically, we hit my target, though not as I had envisioned it.

In many ways it is the clergy of the diocese and their families who become the chief pastoral responsibility of the bishop. The bishop sees them frequently in a variety of settings, and often has the privilege of counseling and praying with them as they face the issues of their own and their parishioners' lives.

Nearly every Sunday brings an official "Episcopal Visitation" to a congregation. That visit will include baptisms, confirmations, and various kinds of reaffirmations of faith. Often it means meeting with the vestry and other congregational leaders. Sometimes there is a Q and A session. And sometimes the bishop is asked to address various specific topics in a forum or meet with a Sunday School class. Frequently the rector will ask the bishop to visit one or more of the congregation's shut-ins. I lost count of the baptisms I performed, but during my not-quite-23 years in office, I confirmed more than 10,000 people and received another 3,000 from other denominations. And I had the privilege of ordaining 218 deacons (including my wife Karen) and 105 men and women to the priesthood and receiving two others from the Roman Catholic Church.

It was always a very special thing for me to see God using the clergy of my diocese in the lives of their parishioners. I recall going with one rector to see a woman who had been confined to a nursing home for many years. She had no family, and no one else ever paid her a visit, but when her priest came calling, her face lit up as if Jesus himself were there. She reminded me of my friend, Addie Woram, who prayed for me so faithfully during my early years of ministry.

During the closing years of the 20th century, and the opening years of the 21st, Central Florida was one of the few dioceses that showed steady growth numerically, financially, and, I believe, spiritually, in a time of increasing controversy and stress in the larger Church.

When we arrived in Orlando, I began an informal "Prayer and Praise" service that met in the Great Hall of the Cathedral on Friday nights. It was modeled on what we had done at Truro, and several of the local clergy joined me in leading it. It usually drew about 100-150 people from the greater Orlando area. And I taught Bible studies every week at Tuesday Luncheons at the Cathedral, again reminiscent of what we had done at Truro.

The Cathedral itself extended a warm welcome to me and my family. The Dean, Harry Sherman, invited me to do a series of Sunday sermons during my first summer in Orlando. I took a fresh look at the Ten Commandments in as many weeks. My thesis was that the Commandments were meant to ensure our freedom, not restrict it. (You don't have to be enslaved to any other gods, controlled by the desires of the flesh, at war with your parents, consumed by lust or envy, etc. Jesus said, "You will know the truth, and the truth will make you free.")[94]

During the year preceding my election, Bishop Folwell had moved the diocesan office from what had originally been a large private home on the shore of one of Winter Park's loveliest lakes to a new location in downtown Orlando. Unfortunately, a planned sale of the former property to a counseling practice was scuttled when the town of Winter Park insisted the building be returned to a single-family residence status. The diocese had hoped the relocation costs would be covered by the sale; instead, it resulted in a more than million-dollar mortgage. The Winter Park house didn't sell, didn't

---

[94]John 8:31. Once again, these sermons can be found on BibleBanquet.com.

sell, didn't sell. Karen and some faithful women marched around the property, anointing it with oil and commanding it to sell. And I asked the whole diocese to join me in a day of prayer that God would lift this unexpected financial burden. My request was scorned by some of the clergy – "You don't really think *that's*, going to help, do you?" – but the property sold within a week. As Ken Medema put it in his lovely little chorus: "Something's gonna happen like the world has never known, when the people of the Lord get down to pray...."[95]

I was asked to make my teaching and preaching (from Truro and now as Bishop) available for distribution, and we began what we called Cathedral Tapes, with Karen as its Administrator. Her office was initially in the Cathedral office building and later it moved to the diocesan office building.

A cathedral is the "Bishop's church." The very word, "cathedral" comes from the Latin word for [the bishop's] "chair." The day-to-day running of a cathedral is usually in the hands of a Dean, who serves at the Bishop's pleasure, but – much more than in any of the other churches in a diocese – the Bishop is "in charge" in his cathedral. In many ways, St. Luke's did become a home for me. I was always there on Christmas and Easter, and most of our ordinations and many diocesan conventions were held there. But there was also strong opposition. Dean Sherman was largely in the Ed Browning camp, and he championed the full inclusion of gays and lesbians in the liturgical life of the Cathedral. A small but determined group of them were openly hostile to both Karen and me. They spoke loudly and disparagingly of us and ridiculed the Tape ministry in particular. One of them began calling me "Your A** Holiness." Another, a member of the choir, even paraded a large monkey puppet dressed as a bishop in the choral procession on Christmas Eve in 1992.

---

[95] Lord, Listen to Your Children, Ken Medema, 1980

Several leaders of the congregation visited Dean Sherman and begged him to intervene and stop this rebellion before it split the Cathedral family apart. When he said he could do nothing about it, they began a financial boycott that shortly forced his resignation. Some cathedral members accused me of orchestrating that effort, but it was well under way before I even learned of it, and those who were behind it were determined to succeed. And they did. Predictably, the Cathedral family was deeply fractured, and my leadership was undermined. This greatly complicated the business of calling a new Dean. The bylaws of the Chapter (the Cathedral vestry) spelled out the process:

> "The Dean shall be elected by the Chapter *on the nomination of the Bishop* and shall continue in office until his resignation, death or removal *by the Bishop* with the consent of a majority of the voting members of the Chapter in accordance with the canons of the Episcopal Church." (Italics added.)

I met with the Chapter, and said, "The calling of a Dean is handled differently in different dioceses. Here, it falls to me to nominate, and you to elect. I can see doing this in at least three different ways. First, I can give you just one name, and you either accept or reject it. If you reject it, I will give you another – and another and another until there is a match. OR, second, I can give you a short list of names and ask you to choose one of them. OR, third, *you* can give *me* a short list, and I will pick from among them – and then you will have to confirm that choice."

The Chapter agreed to take this third approach and asked the congregation to begin submitting names. Unbeknownst to any of the members, I submitted one name myself, that of G. Richard Lobs, Rector of St. Mark's in Geneva, Illinois. I had known Rick and his wife Donna, a Deacon, for many years, and I thought Rick was ideally suited to restore the equilibrium of the damaged congregation.

Over the next few months, I met regularly with the Chapter, and their trust in me seemed to be returning. When they submitted their list of three names, Rick's was on it. I surprised everyone by saying, "I'd like to change the rules." Change the rules! At this late date? They were extremely wary. What was I going to do? Having invited the Chapter to be part of the selection process, was I going to take it back as my own prerogative? "No." I said, "Any of these three men would make a fine Dean. I want you to make the choice yourselves." With a great expression of relief and appreciation, they chose Rick Lobs – who went on to be one of the premier cathedral deans in the Episcopal Church.

The conflict at the Cathedral had given it the reputation as a place to be avoided, a scarecrow of sorts. When Rick arrived a couple of months later, I invited him to address our diocesan convention. He adapted an illustration from Hannah Hurnard, author of *Hinds' Feet on High Places*: "A wise bird knows that a scarecrow is simply an advertisement. There are scarecrows only in carefully tended gardens. A wise bird sees scarecrows as an invitation to a banquet." In summarizing its history, the Cathedral reports on its website: "Dean Lobs brought the Cathedral's worship to new heights of glory and ushered in an enduring era of excellence in preaching and teaching of God's Word." In retrospect, I am grateful not only for the choice itself, but for the way it unfolded.

One of the great pleasures of our time in Central Florida was spending time with our youngest daughter, Jessica. It seemed to me that Kathy had been the focus of our early years, John had made many international mission trips with me during our Truro time, and finally it was Jessica's turn. Her considerable musical talent, especially her lovely singing voice, was emerging and she developed a great interest in all things musical. We subscribed to the "Broadway in Orlando" series and one highlight was a special backstage visit with Carol Channing who encouraged Jess to pursue music as the early direction of her life. She majored in music education at Florida State University, and then spent several years as a music instructor and married Bruce Jones in 2000. They have two musically gifted children, and Jessica is now ordained and serving in the ACNA while living in the Jacksonville area.

The Diocese of Central Florida sponsored some wonderful events during our time there, including a visit by the 103rd Archbishop of Canterbury, George L. Carey (who was kind enough to write forewords to both my *Anointed by the Spirit* and the second edition of *Our Anglican Heritage*). We also did a lot of fun things like clergy conferences and retreats in various oceanside hotels. And Karen and I hosted a diocesan-wide Open House in our home each year just before Christmas. We hired a group of singers who wore 19th century apparel and sang the great choruses and carols of the holiday season. (We did have one horrific Open House moment, when the caterer poured hot liquid chocolate into the kitchen sink, where – of course – it congealed and stopped our plumbing entirely. So while our guests mingled, Roto-Rooter cleared our pipes, and while we were horrified, no one else even seemed to notice.)

I was grateful that we had very few disciplinary problems during my time in office. One terrible exception involved a Deacon who was hired by Walt Disney World to do services at the resort's Wedding Pavilion. A deacon can only officiate at weddings with his bishop's permission, and of course this man had no such permission, so he posed as a priest to do this. He was performing weddings for people he had never met, giving them no pre-marital counseling, and often doing second, third, or even fourth marriages – which would have required still further permissions. But he had none. Technically that meant that *none of the weddings he performed were legal,* although to my knowledge none was ever questioned. We discovered all this when the chancellor from another diocese booked a Disney wedding package for herself, and she discovered she had been assigned to a "priest" who asked her none of the questions he should have asked. (Our deacon hastily departed the Episcopal Church when he was found out.)

One of our congregations called a rector from far-away Hawaii, only to have him return to the Aloha State just a few months after arriving in Central Florida. Bringing him and his family all that way had been a huge expense for a small congregation, and the parish – and especially its vestry – was deeply hurt, puzzled, and angry when he left so soon after coming. I met with a very dispirited group of leaders and said, "Before God enables you to move on, you must forgive Rich for what seems a terrible betrayal of your love and trust. I'm asking that each of you say the words, 'I forgive you, Rich,' just as if he were sitting with us here at this table." It was a struggle, but finally every one of the vestry members repeated those words. Then I said, "I think I know who your next rector will be." And I recommended Ron Robison, who had been on the calling committee that invited me to Truro, and who was just then completing his studies at the Virginia Theological Seminary. They interviewed him, and it was, indeed, a match. "Robbie" had a wonderfully fruitful ministry there over the next several years, and the parish grew to be one of the two most completely integrated churches in the diocese.

Central Florida's "companion relationship" with the Diocese of Honduras – in one of the poorest countries in the world, but one in which the Church is thriving – was, and is, by far the longest standing such relationship between any two dioceses in the Anglican world. We in Central Florida were able to give much materially, and receive much spiritually, from our brothers and sisters in Honduras.

One of my greatest joys was sharing with clergy, vestries,

and congregations some of the lessons we had learned about church growth, giving, outreach, decision-making, vision-casting, church planting, and mutual accountability. And in 2004, I had the enormous pleasure of ordaining my own wife, Karen, to the sacred diaconate after four years of studies at The Institute for Christian Studies, a rigorous diocesan school. Karen did her preparation under Cathedral Dean Rick Lobs. Rick insisted on Karen doing a service project before becoming a deacon, and when he asked her if, by any chance, she could paint, she said, yes, she could paint. She thought he meant changing the color of some walls. No - he meant painting a *mural* – in a 16 x 8-foot storeroom on unfinished walls. It took her a year to complete the project, but it remains one of the great attractions of the Cathedral of St. Luke in Orlando, Florida.

The runner-up in my election was Bishop Folwell's Canon to the Ordinary (chief assistant) Tom Downs. To nearly everyone's surprise, I asked Tom to stay on as my Canon, and he accepted. Tom's knowledge of the diocese, and his familiarity with the clergy were very helpful to me as I began my new responsibilities. Tom was with me for the first two years of my episcopacy, before he became rector of St. Paul's Church in Albany, Georgia. When Tom left, I asked the Rev. Ernie Bennett, rector of St. Andrews, Ft. Pierce, to become Canon. Ernie served with me for the rest of my time in Central Florida and helped me build what I think was one of the strongest staff teams in the Episcopal Church. We began every day in the small chapel in Diocesan House that we called "The Oratorio," with a time of worship, scripture and prayer. We frequently had lunch together, and we became true friends and partners in ministry.

In moving to Central Florida, Karen and I had to sell our getaway home at Lake of the Woods and find a permanent home in Orlando. Both tasks were challenging, and both became great confirmations that what was happening was of God. One of Northern Virginia's top realtors was a member of Truro. She advertised our lake property in Fredericksburg, in the DC area, and nationally. But it didn't sell. Meanwhile, we looked for a home in Orlando. We found one on Jessamine Lane, about ten minutes from the Cathedral, but it was far out of our price range. Our Orlando realtor suggested we put in a very low bid, knowing the sellers would counter, and we could negotiate from there. We did that…and then I realized our "low" bid was as high as we could possibly go. The sellers rejected our offer just as our realtor had predicted. But I had to say that we could go no higher. We looked at alternatives and were about to bid on a house in nearby Oviedo that was not nearly as nice but seemed to be the best we could do. Suddenly our realtor called. The folks on Jessamine Lane had just phoned her. They said they had prayed about it, and they heard the Lord say they were to "sell to the Howes without hassle." They assumed that meant they were to accept our offer. Amazingly, in the 24 hours since we visited, someone else had viewed their home and offered their full asking price. But they accepted *our* offer of $40,000 less – for people they had never met previously – because the Lord told them to. (We didn't even know they were believers, but we were certainly glad to discover they were.)

Several weeks later we learned that the house we had nearly purchased in Oviedo was being torn down. A crack in the foundation could not be repaired and the house had to be destroyed. When I told Bruce Scott, my builder friend in Fairfax, about it, he said, "There's a saying in the construction industry that 'a problem in the foundation will follow you all the way to the roof.'" God kept us from a terrible investment.

Meanwhile, our lake house in Virginia *didn't* sell, didn't sell, didn't sell, despite our fervent prayer. Days turned into weeks, and weeks into months. We were wrestling with two mortgages. And huge anxiety. One Sunday morning, on the way to a visitation, as I was praying about it, that familiar voice of the Lord said very clearly: *"Sell it yourself."* And I argued: just how can I do that when a top realtor has not been able to?

Then I remembered that a friend from Truro had said he would love to buy the house but would have to wait about a year. I called and asked him, "If the Diocesan Board here in Florida were to give you a one-year loan, would you be interested in buying the Lake of the Woods house?" He said he would. The Board agreed. So, he bought the house, paying a *lower* rate of interest than he could have gotten from any bank. The Diocesan Board lent him the money and made *more* in interest for that one year than they could have made from a bank. And Karen and I sold the house without having to pay any realtor's fees. A remarkable combination that was a huge reassurance that God had planned the whole thing with great care.

I found I wasn't finished with Virginia, however. The New Life Fellowship, which met on Friday mornings in the National Presbyterian Church in Washington, DC, asked me to take over as its principal teacher in 1997. For many years, Terry Fullam had flown south from Connecticut to DC to teach nearly every week. But a stroke forced him to discontinue doing that. So, for about four years I began flying north each week to meet with usually about 150 or so who attended. I stayed with daughter Kathy and her family on Thursday nights and drove into the District the next morning. It was a wonderful chance to reconnect with her and minister to some exceptional Washington Christians.

I had become a member of the House of Bishops at a moment when it was changing dramatically. Barbara Harris, the first woman bishop in the history of Anglicanism, had been elected in Massachusetts just six months earlier. This was such a novelty that at one point the Presiding Bishop accidentally addressed her as "Sir." At my first meeting of the House, the bishops were seated at long tables, all facing front, in the order in which we had been consecrated. But by the very next meeting that practice was abandoned, never to be resumed. We now sat at round tables, deliberately mixed in terms of age, experience, geographical location, and – probably – perceived theological positions.

We spent what seemed to me an inordinate amount of time discussing racial division and reconciliation and listening to long-ago speeches of Martin Luther King, Jr., who had been assassinated more than two decades previously. I wondered whether our whole discussion was really about something else altogether, namely our growing division over sexuality, and specifically homosexuality. Was this endless discussion of racial inequality actually a sort of code for advancing the cause of greater sexual diversity?

Becoming an Episcopal bishop in 1989 meant crossing swords with Jack Spong, the flamboyant and controversial bishop of Newark. Even before Spong published his "Twelve Points for Reform,"[96] he was seeking to "reinterpret" virtually every major tenet of the Christian Faith, from the virgin birth to the resurrection, from Jesus' divinity to the very being of God. Sadly, it seemed to most people this was not so much a *reinterpretation* as an outright *denial* of orthodoxy. But Spong remained a bishop in good standing. He became one of the principal spokesmen for changing the Church's understanding of sexuality, contending for the ordination of non-celibate gay and lesbian men and women and for the blessing of same-sex unions.

I met Bishop Spong when I was advocating for correcting the church's position on abortion. I told him that though I disagreed with much of what he was saying, I found his monthly column always worth reading. When I was elected Bishop Coadjutor, he sent me a pair of purple booties, hand-knitted by his mother. He said she

---

[96]Originally published in *The Voice*, the monthly newsletter of the Diocese of Newark in 1998, and subsequently elaborated in his book *A New Christianity for a New World*, Harper, 2001

had given him a pair when he became a bishop a decade previously, and she had knitted a pair for every bishop elected in the intervening years (though, for whatever reason, I was the last one to receive that unusual gift).

Spong and I were on opposite sides of most of the questions coming before the House of Bishops, and he several times called me his "nemesis." Once he greeted me with the question, "Is it you, you troubler of Israel?" (An interesting question, in that he was quoting King Ahab's greeting to the prophet Elijah. Elijah's response was, "It is not I who has troubled Israel; but you and your father's house, because you have forsaken the commandments of the Lord and followed the Baals."[97])

I was invited to debate Spong at the Virginia Theological Seminary in February 1992. I began by referring to the marriage service in the Episcopal Church's *Book of Common Prayer*:

> "The bond and covenant of marriage was established by God in creation, and our Lord Jesus Christ adorned this manner of life by his presence and first miracle at a wedding in Cana of Galilee. It signifies to us the mystery of the union between Christ and his Church, and Holy Scripture commends it to be honored among all people."[98]

I said: "The service continues by *defining* marriage as 'the union of husband and wife in heart, body, and mind.'" (That, by the way, continues to be the Church's official position even though the General Convention authorized same-sex "marriages" in 2015).

I continued:

---

[97] 1 Kings 18:17-18
[98] The Celebration and Blessing of a Marriage, The Book of Common Prayer, p. 423.

"My quarrel with Bishop Spong is not over whether or not we have drawn the right conclusions from a few obscure references to sexuality in the book of Leviticus. I'm objecting to his wholesale setting aside of the entire witness of Scripture and tradition: the Church's received teaching that sexual intimacy is appropriate only within the commitment of holy matrimony – one man, one woman, faithful to each other in Christ....

"That's a high standard, and few of us have unblemished records with regard to it... Clearly there's no room for condemnation of failure, for we are all failures. But neither is it helpful to commend what God has forbidden. Somewhere I read that 'whoever relaxes one of the least of these commandments, and teaches others so, shall be called least in the kingdom of heaven.' (Matthew 5:19)

"Bishop Spong's argument becomes finally that because one is born with a homosexual orientation, or an irresistible tendency to develop one, it is cruel, unjust, unloving, and ultimately unchristian for us to deny that person the 'right' to express that orientation in sexual behavior. But that is a non-sequitur. To argue from an orientation to a behavior is to leave out our fallen-ness. This world – and all of the people in it – has been sufficiently corrupted and broken by sin that we can find folks wanting to do just about anything imaginable."

We made a recording of the debate available through Cathedral Tapes, and I appended a personal "afterword" – some further reflections clearly added at a later date. When Bishop Spong learned of this, he accused me of having altered the debate itself – which I did *not* – and he demanded we stop distributing the tape. We agreed to his demand, but he continued making that accusation in one of his books and at least two of his diocesan newspaper columns - even though he knew it was false.

Some in the audience said I won the debate that night, but over the past four decades Spong's position has clearly won the day in the Episcopal Church. The Church's revision of its understanding of sexuality has been the major factor in the departure of so many of its clergy and bishops, congregations, and dioceses. Each of us must make up our own mind about a question like this. Obviously, many people think Jack Spong was right. Nearly all of the bishops remaining in the Episcopal Church apparently think so. But if Spong was right, the whole of our Christian tradition has been wrong. The Roman Catholic Church is wrong. The Orthodox Churches are wrong. The evangelicals are wrong. Scripture itself must be wrong. And, of course, that would mean Jesus was also wrong, for he quoted the Book of Genesis, when he asked, "Have you not read that the one who made them at the beginning 'made them male and female,' and said, 'For this reason a man shall leave his father and mother and be joined to his wife, and the two shall become one flesh'?" (Matthew 19:4-5). God invented marriage. He meant it for a man and a woman to be united in a relationship that reflects his own love affair with his ancient covenant people and Jesus' marriage to his Bride, the Church.

I was part of two very long-shot legal attempts to change the Church's trajectory, neither of which succeeded. In 1996 eleven bishops brought charges against Walter Righter, Assistant Bishop to Jack Spong in Newark, for ordaining an openly non-celibate gay man to the priesthood. The Trial Court determined that the Church's teaching regarding sexuality was not part of its "core doctrine," and that such teaching was subject to change, and Bishop Righter was exonerated. Sadly, at least three of the nine bishops on the court had performed similar ordinations in their own dioceses, but they refused to recuse themselves.

The following year, 1997, Bishop William Wantland of Eau Clair, Wisconsin, spearheaded an effort to protect an island of orthodoxy within a drifting Church by incorporating the original, formal name of TEC – which had never been incorporated previously – "the Protestant Episcopal Church in the United States of America" (PECUSA) and attaching to it a very clear statement of faith and establishing a board of trustees. He argued that regardless of whatever novel decisions others might make regarding these issues, there would then be a place within the Church where orthodox Episcopalians could stand.

I supported that effort until Presiding Bishop Ed Browning denounced it as "an attempt to violate the Church's right and need to protect its name," and of "creating confusion within the Church and the wider public generally." That's the exact opposite of what we were trying to do. We wanted to "protect" a place within TEC for those who opposed the confusion being created by the Church changing its teaching and practice. We were trying to help orthodox Episcopalians find a way of staying *in* the Church, not a way to *leave* it. But, when I saw the way our effort was being interpreted, I withdrew from PECUSA immediately. Bishop Wantland's attempt ultimately collapsed.

Increasingly I faced criticism from those who were leaving: "How can you stay in TEC as it becomes ever more heretical?" My answer was always, "I have made promises that I will uphold the doctrine and discipline of the Episcopal Church '*as this Church has received them.*'"[99] I said, "Others may depart from what we have received, but until or unless I am commanded by TEC to do what God forbids or forbidden to do what God commands, I will not leave."

---

[99] See The Ordination of a Priest, and The Ordination of a Deacon, *The Book of Common* Prayer, pp. 526 and 538.

In some ways, the sexuality battles dominated my episcopacy – because they dominated the Episcopal Church. In 2003 Gene Robinson was elected Bishop Coadjutor of New Hampshire. Gene was the first openly non-celibate gay man to be consecrated Bishop in any major Christian denomination that retains the historic episcopate. Despite our deep opposition to each other's theological positions, Gene and I developed a respectful personal friendship, and we were both often sought for comments on the "issues" by members of the press.

Interestingly – and surprising to many people - I also maintained a friendly rivalry with Louie Crew, who had championed the "full inclusion of gay and lesbian persons" in TEC since 1974. I saw this as an ominous development and preached about it during my last year at St. Stephen's, a sermon that was printed in *The Living Church*, then reprinted in several other publications. Louie wrote to me, and we began a correspondence that lasted for about a year. I told Louie I was praying for him. When he said he was returning the favor, I commented, "How confusing for God!" Louie and I disagreed vehemently, but we were always respectful and cordial with each other. When we ended our correspondence, realizing neither of us was going to change the other's mind, Louie said, "I want you to know that nobody, coming from where you are coming from, has ever treated me as graciously as you have." We later served on a couple of national and General Convention committees together.

Most of the "mainline" denominations in the United States have been losing members at an alarming rate since the mid-sixties, but for the Episcopal Church the departures increased exponentially. In 1966, at its highest point, TEC reported it had 3,647,297 members. By 2022 (the most recent year for which statistics have been published) that number had dropped to 1,584,785 – a loss of over 56% of its membership. That picture is further complicated by the fact that the average age of today's Episcopalian is sixty-nine, so many statisticians are anticipating the total collapse of the Episcopal Church in about another two decades.

Meanwhile, the rest of the Anglican Communion has been drawn into the conflict, with nearly half of its member provinces (national churches) declaring they are in "impaired" or "broken" communion with TEC over sexuality disagreements.[100]

During my time in Central Florida, we weathered two very difficult seasons of "disaffiliation" in which a total of eleven of our congregations split. Initially they tried to persuade me to lead their departure from TEC. I was adamantly against doing that. Twice - first as a Deacon, then as a Priest - I pledged to "be loyal to the doctrine, discipline, and worship of Christ as [the Episcopal] Church has received them." Once – as a Bishop – I had promised to "guard the faith, unity, and discipline of the [Episcopal] Church." Until or unless TEC were to officially renounce its own teaching, I would not abandon it. I believed my calling was to guard those who wished to remain Episcopalian, but also to make provision for those who wished to leave for conscience's sake.

When the clergy and wardens of those eleven congregations finally realized I would not champion their cause they asked for a meeting with me in which they declared their intention to depart. "We don't have a quarrel with you, Bishop, or with the Diocese of Central Florida," their spokesman declared. "Our quarrel is with the Episcopal Church. We have taken vows to remain true to the teachings of Jesus and the scriptures, and TEC is rewriting everything the Bible says about sexuality, marriage, and what it

---

[100]There are presently 42 autonomous provinces, and 5 "extra provincial" national or local churches in the Anglican Communion, making it the third largest denominational body in Christendom, after the Roman Catholic Church and the Churches of (Eastern) Orthodoxy. Traditionally, "being in communion" has been defined as "being in communion with a bishop who is in communion with the Archbishop of Canterbury." But in this present season of "impaired communion," the majority of the provinces say they *are* in communion with ACNA, but they are *not* in full communion with The Episcopal Church.

means to be made in the image of God. We cannot continue being part of this church as it becomes ever more apostate."

Similar things were happening in nearly every diocese of the Episcopal Church. Many clergy and congregations wanted to *leave*, and in nearly every case there were prolonged, hugely expensive lawsuits, as they tried to take the church property with them. Jeff Walton of the Institute on Religion and Democracy estimated that the total legal expenses of the Episcopal Church against its departing dioceses and parishes was approximately $52 million, and that did not include the amounts spend by dioceses against departing parishes. And, of course, the amounts spent by those wanting to leave TEC were in many cases even greater.[101]

Nearly all of the legal battles were decided in favor of TEC – that is, the property remained part of the Episcopal Church, not the departing congregation. This was a very difficult point, especially in those cases where the great majority of parishioners wanted to leave TEC. They felt they had been paying the bills for many years, and the real property should go with them. But the courts were usually correct because in nearly every case there were some parishioners who did not want to leave, and they had a claim upon the property as well. Usually, the properties were originally purchased and built with the help of the diocese, and so long as members of those congregations wanted to continue being part of TEC, they had a right to do so, and to do so in their historic church buildings.

The leaders of our eleven congregations pressed me: "What will you do if we decide to leave?" I replied, "I will say to you what is said at the close of nearly every worship service, 'Go in peace to love and serve the Lord.'" And, so, in each of them a portion of the congregation left to form a new church, sometimes retaining the former name, but now calling it *Anglican* rather than *Episcopal*. Of

---

[101] Institute on Religion and Democracy Blog, August 31, 2021

those who left, all but one have finally become affiliated with either the Anglican Mission in America (AMiA) or the Anglican Church in North America (ACNA) – both of which seek to be orthodox alternatives to TEC. Gloria Dei in Cocoa, voted to become an independent community church, and has since closed down.

The Anglican Mission in America was formed in January 2000, when the Archbishop of Rwanda, Emmanuel Kolini, and the Archbishop of Southeast Asia, Moses Tay, ordained two American priests, John Rodgers, (former Dean/President of Trinity School for Ministry), and Chuck Murphy, (rector of All Saints Church, Pawleys Island, South Carolina) as "Missionary Bishops" to re-evangelize The Episcopal Church. AMiA was initially a full member of the Anglican Church in North America, but later defined itself as a "Ministry Partner" of ACNA, and since 2012 it has sought oversight from other Anglican Communion provinces.

The Anglican Church in North America was founded in 2009 by former members of the Episcopal Church in the United States and the Anglican Church of Canada who were deeply disturbed by the departure of their churches from their historic positions on human sexuality and the Gospel itself. ACNA is not officially part of the Anglican Communion – that is, it is not recognized as a constituent member province by the Archbishop of Canterbury - but the majority of other provinces in the Communion say they are in full communion with ACNA, even while they repudiate communion with TEC.

ACNA incorporates the full spectrum of orthodox Anglicanism, not only in the United States and Canada, but also in ten congregations in Mexico and mission churches in Guatemala and Cuba. It includes Anglo-Catholic, charismatic, and evangelical theological expressions and it is committed to the "dual integrities" of those who support the ordination of women and those who oppose it. Ordained women serve as priests and deacons in some dioceses but may not do so in others. Women may not serve as bishops, however, in any dioceses of ACNA. In some dioceses the disagreement over women's ordination is seen as "impaired communion." ACNA holds that marriage is between one man and one woman. It is strongly pro-life, and it opposes both abortion and euthanasia. Its congregations own their property. It is deeply committed to evangelism and church planting.

ACNA's first Archbishop was Robert Duncan, former Episcopal Bishop of Pittsburgh, who was succeeded in 2014 by Foley Beach, formerly Bishop of the Anglican Diocese of the South, and before that Rector of St. Alban's Episcopal Church in Monroe, Georgia. On the issues of sexuality and the Gospel itself, the Anglican Church in North America is solidly orthodox. As of 2022 it reported 977 congregations and 130,000 members.

As AMiA and ACNA were both taking hold, legal warfare and these hugely expensive lawsuits were ripping the Episcopal Church apart in nearly every diocese. Central Florida avoided such battles almost entirely. We did go into court-ordered mediation twice, and both times we were able to work out amicable settlements.

During this time of upheaval, as Bishops and Archbishops around the world declared they were no longer in communion with the Episcopal Church, I was one of several orthodox American bishops who exchanged letters and phone calls with, and finally made repeated visits to, Lambeth Palace to meet first with Archbishop George Carey, and then with his successor, Archbishop Rowan Williams. Our concern was *How do we ensure that orthodox bishops and dioceses remain in good standing in the Communion while the Episcopal Church as a whole seems to be departing from it?*

Archbishop Williams sent me a letter in 2007 and invited me to share it widely. He wrote,

> "Any Diocese [continuing to uphold the teaching of the Anglican Communion] remains clearly in communion with Canterbury and the mainstream of the Communion, whatever may be the longer-term result for others in The Episcopal Church. The organ of union with the wider Church is the Bishop and the Diocese rather than the Provincial structure as such… I should feel a great deal happier, I must say, if those who are most eloquent for a traditionalist view in the United States showed a fuller understanding of the need to regard the Bishop and the Diocese as the primary locus of ecclesial identity rather than the abstract reality of the 'National Church.'"

That was the uneasy place we were in. Central Florida was an island of refuge in a sea of uncertainty. We were in communion with Canterbury and most of the Anglican world, while much of the Episcopal Church was drifting. We had lost portions of several congregations, but we were on good terms with those who had left. And we were rebuilding the congregations that had been fractured by their departure.

As the General Convention of 2012 was approaching my own mandatory retirement would be at hand just two years later. I began to question whether an orthodox believer could ever be elected as my successor and confirmed by the current House of Bishops. I concluded that I should step down from episcopal responsibilities before the Convention acted. We began the process, which led to the election of Gregory O. Brewer, who had previously served as rector in one of Central Florida's parishes, and who had helped me lead our Prayer and Praise services when I first came to Orlando. Greg was elected in November 2011, and consecrated on March 24, 2012. And so ended my time in office. But not before two of our priests, who were in the final stages of their lives, asked to see me. I was deeply moved that both of them somehow found the strength to dress in their clericals and get up from their deathbeds to greet and pray with their bishop one more time before he retired.

Greg initially said he wanted me to continue as an Assistant Bishop in Central Florida, but sadly that never actually developed. I still received many invitations to visit our congregations on Sundays, but it was not in an official diocesan capacity.

As I had anticipated, the General Convention voted on July 12, 2012, to authorize the blessing of same-sex unions, initially with a conscience clause barring penalties for bishops who would not permit them in their dioceses. Then in 2015 TEC approved "trial rites" for the marriage of same-sex couples. And in 2018 it became mandatory that *every diocesan bishop permit such marriages in his/her diocese.* Those (few) still opposed were to place the clergy and parishes desiring them under the auspices of bishops who would approve them. And by 2020 every diocesan bishop in the Church had complied but one. Bishop William Love, of the Diocese of Albany said he could not submit to this new teaching.

A disciplinary panel ruled in October 2020 that he violated church law by prohibiting the same-sex marriage rite approved by the General Convention in 2018. Four months later Bishop Love resigned from TEC and announced he was joining the Anglican Church in North America.

For me, this was the breaking point. It didn't affect me directly, as I was no longer in office, it meant I could no longer have functioned as a bishop had I not already stepped down. It was, finally, the very thing I had so long resisted. In that decision, the Episcopal Church redefined both marriage and the nature of the episcopacy. A bishop could no longer be a bishop as had been historically understood. I sent a letter to Presiding Bishop Michael

Curry requesting release from the ordained ministry of the Episcopal Church. I said:

> "It has been my honor and pleasure to serve in the ordained ministry of the Episcopal Church for 53 years, and I have tried with all my strength to do so well.
>
> "Over these five decades TEC has changed dramatically, and I have been deeply involved in some of its most notable struggles. But my position has always been that unless I were ordered to do what God forbids, or forbidden to do what he commands, I would have no reason to consider leaving...
>
> "However, the charges that have been brought against Bishop Love of Albany force me to reexamine that position. Bishop Love has directed the clergy of Albany not to officiate at marriage ceremonies that are not in accord with the liturgy and rubrics of *The Book of Common Prayer*. And for this he is accused of violating the discipline of the Episcopal Church.
>
> "Since I am no longer in diocesan authority, this does not affect me directly. But it does indicate that TEC has changed its doctrine, discipline, and worship to the point that I am asking you to transfer me to the jurisdiction of the Anglican Church in North America.
>
> "Please know that I will ever remain your friend and the friend of TEC. I give thanks for your witness, ministry, and leadership, and you will remain in my prayers."

Bishop Curry said he could not transfer me, but with the consent of his Advisory Council, he most graciously released me from the ordained ministry of the Episcopal Church. Almost simultaneously Archbishop Foley Beach received Karen and me as retired clergy in the Anglican Church in North America. And he wrote the very gracious Foreword to this book. Thank you, sir.

ACNA is the Church I had so hoped TEC would become.

Chapter 9

A New Beginning at Lake of the Woods

Now Joshua was old and advanced in years; and the Lord said to him, 'You are old and advanced in years, and very much of the land remains to be possessed' (Joshua 13:1).

The morning I was to defend my doctoral thesis for the Graduate Theological Foundation I received a call from Creation House with the happy news that they would publish it as a book entitled *Anointed by the Spirit.* Subtitle: *A study of the ministry of Jesus and his followers.* I wanted to share the central truths that God has been unfolding to me over the past half century:

- Jesus was and is both fully human and fully divine,
- The key to his ministry was not primarily in his *divinity* but in his *anointing.*
- He operated in the power of the Holy Spirit.
- The "signs and wonders" that he performed were gifts or manifestations of the Holy Spirit, and
- That same Spirit-anointing is the birthright of every Christian.

Jesus called himself (among many other things) "the light of the world." (John 8:12) But he also said to his disciples, "*You* are the light of the world." (Matthew 5:14) And he said they (and we) are to "let our light shine" so that other people will see the good things we do and "give glory to our Father in heaven." (Matthew 5:16). *We* are to do good things, but the *Holy Spirit* enables us to do them. *We* are to be the light of the world, but the *Holy Spirit* is the "fuel" that keeps our light burning.

St. Paul said the key to living the Christian life is being "filled with the Spirit." (Ephesians 5:18). The verb is *plerousthe*, and technically it is a present passive imperative verb – literally "be being filled," or "be filled and go on being filled" moment by moment, day by day. Jesus said that if we know how to give good gifts to our children, *how much more* will the heavenly Father give the Holy Spirit to those who ask him." (Luke 11:13)

The joy of my life has been knowing Christ, sharing him with others, and experiencing something of the supernatural power of God. But now I had stepped down from my episcopal responsibilities. I was still often being asked to visit various congregations on Sunday mornings, but I had the sense that God had something more for me to do. Some friends told me that the Lake of the Woods Church back in Virginia was looking for a new Senior Pastor. After three years of "retirement" I applied for the job.

Beginning with forty-three candidates, the Committee watched and listened to video and audio recordings of sermons, and narrowed the field to seven, then three finalists. There was, initially, some wariness at the thought of a 72-year-old Episcopal bishop becoming the Pastor of a multi-denominational community church.

The Search Committee asked me four *very* pointed questions:

1. As a multi-denominational church, we embrace different worship styles and practices… Please discuss your experience with traditional, blended, and contemporary worship services. Are you more comfortable leading worship in one type of venue or another?

2. Our new Senior Pastor must understand and fully support LOWC's organizational structure…[which was *very* different from what I had known in Episcopal circles, either at the

parish or the diocesan level]. Please describe how you believe your leadership style and prior experience will make you an effective Senior Pastor in LOWC with an organizational structure of shared authority between clergy and lay leaders.

3. Over the last few years, the Lord has led LOWC to expand our vision to include concerted efforts in community missions… In what ways would you be supportive of this vision?

4. What functions do you believe small groups can serve? Specifically…how do you see small group ministry functioning as a means of discipleship, evangelism, community missions, and assimilation of seekers and new members?

Apparently they liked my answers, because the Committee – including the outgoing Senior Pastor (!) – voted unanimously to recommend me to the congregation. They brought Karen and me to Locust Grove for me to preach and meet people on October 4, 2015. (Some of the members remembered us from our time at the lake so many years before.)

On November first, the congregation voted to call me, and on my birthday, three days later, I sent my acceptance. In my letter to them I mentioned that "J.B. Phillips' translation of First Thessalonians contains this intriguing sentence: *'We know that God not only loves you but has selected you for a special purpose.'* (I Thess.1:4)." I said: "Those words resonate in my mind and spirit as I think of the unique calling and ministry of the Lake of the Woods Church." I added, "As many of you know, Karen and I had a home at the Lake back in the 1980s, so it will really be a homecoming for us. We are looking forward to catching up with old friends and meeting so many new ones."

The Lake of the Woods Church strives to concentrate on what all Christians, coming from so many different backgrounds, have in common, and not let denominational differences stand in the way of fellowship, worship, or outreach.

On Sundays there are three quite different worship services:

- <u>Traditional</u> – which feels pretty much like a Congregational or Methodist service, with vestments, hymn books, organ and full choir.

- <u>Contemporary</u> – which is informal, and uses guitars, drums, keyboard, overhead projection screens and a small singing group; and

- <u>Blended</u> – which is sort of a combination of the other two. And interestingly, there is a Wednesday evening communion service right out of the Episcopal *Book of Common Prayer* (slightly abbreviated).

Baptism is both for infants, in church, using a font, and for adults, by immersion, in the lake (in the spring, when it becomes warm enough, and in the fall before it gets too chilly).

After being in Florida for almost 27 years, it was delightful to discover that several families we knew at Truro had moved to Lake of the Woods in their retirement and they were all very active in the church. Some were serving on the Board of Elders, and several were leading house groups patterned on the Shepherd Groups we developed in Fairfax. The President of the Lake of the Woods Association was a close friend from Truro days, and many former parishioners were in various service organizations in the area.

LOWC has a greater hands-on outreach ministry than any congregation I have ever known, with mission trips close by and sometimes to the far corners of the world. It has a deep special relationship with a sister congregation in Navajo Nation in Arizona. Nearly every summer the church sends teams of adults and teenagers to teach and disciple and to work on special building projects there.

There is also a very strong outreach to the local community. LOWC has established free medical and dental clinics serving the uninsured. And it has significantly reached out to the children in nearby schools - by providing supplies each fall and lunch programs throughout the year. It's after-school Good News Clubs are welcomed by principals and the school board. (I know of nowhere else in the country where churches have an entrée to the public schools like the one Lake of the Woods Church has in Locust Grove.) Until it had to close during the Covid pandemic, LOWC ran a five-day-a-week Child Care Center and an after-school program serving both the church and the community. And the Lake of the Woods television channel broadcasts the church's worship services without charge to its viewers.

Frequent "Home Helps" projects serve the elderly and infirm without charge, whether they are members of LOWC, members of some other church, or members of no church at all.

Perhaps the most impressive thing about the church is the way it trains older kids to teach and mentor younger ones. Year after year the "big guys" help the "little guys" learn what it means to follow Jesus.

The biggest difference between LOWC and the churches I served previously is in its governance. The Board of Elders at the church has a very high level of responsibility for decision-making. This often means decisions take longer than they do when "the buck stops" with the rector. But it is often a relief to have that responsibility shared with others.

God called together a remarkable pastoral staff to lead this lovely church. During my time there the team included an Anglican bishop (me), a United Methodist pastor, two Baptist pastors, a non-denominationally ordained pastor, and a Roman Catholic Administrator.

My role focused primarily on preaching and teaching and mentoring the younger men. I "signed-on" for three to five years and ended up staying for six. In the fall of 2021, I told the Board and then the congregation that the time had come for me to step down. It was our hope that Karen and I could spend more time with our family – our eldest, Kathy, and her children and grandchildren who live nearby in Virginia, and John and Jessica and their families in Florida.

As I was writing my letter of resignation, a notification popped up on my computer that a lovely condominium apartment in Orange Park, Florida on the St. Johns River had just come available. It was exactly what we had been hoping to find, and two days later we bought it. Over the past few years, we have been able to spend about half of our time in Virginia and the other half in Florida.

Back in 1981, David Barrett published a huge and amazing book called *The World Christian Encyclopedia*. It was an exhaustive study of what was happening virtually everywhere in the world of Christendom. Someone wants to know what the churches are like in Sri Lanka? Or Bolivia? Or Taiwan? It was there in Barrett's book. On the very first page he brought us to the bottom line. In 1981 there were a total of 20,800 denominations all calling themselves Christian.

But, as shocking as that was, when the second edition came out 20 years later (now a huge two-volume set) that number had grown to 34,000, almost double in two decades. There now have to be more than 50,000 denominations all calling themselves Christian. Having lived through the extremely painful splintering of the Episcopal Church, I know first-hand that sometimes divisions are unavoidable. Sadly there *are* issues that must separate us.

But I am reminded of a parable attributed to "Mr. Pentecost," David du Plessis, whom I met at that great closing eucharist in Canterbury Cathedral so many years ago. He said the Christian Church in all its many divisions is like a great duck pond where the ducks are separated from each other by fences in the water. The Baptist ducks are in one corner, dunking each other under the water. The Roman Catholic ducks are in another corner, sprinkling each other with water. Some sections of the pond are very crowded, some less so. But when God sends the rain the whole pond rises, the fences disappear, and the ducks can swim together. And, of course, the rain is a symbol of the Holy Spirit.

May God send the rain upon his Church!

Chapter 10

Tying Up Some Loose Ends

And what more should I say? For time would fail me to finish all the stories (Hebrews 11:32).

At the end of Johnny Carson's last appearance on *The Tonight Show* they showed a montage of him coming through the curtain again and again as he had done for 30 years. And then they cut to Johnny himself, who said, "If I could, magically, somehow – that tape you just saw – make it run backwards, I'd like to do it all over again."

As I cruise past my 81st birthday, I can't *quite* say that. There are a few notable bits I would certainly do differently or leave out entirely. But really, only a few. Overall, it has been an amazing journey, and I can only offer heartfelt thanks and praise to God.

Let me close with a few bits and pieces about my family.

<u>Karen</u>

At the top of the list of things for which I give thanks is the amazing woman who has shared over sixty of these years with me. Karen carried the lion's share of financial responsibility during the early years of our marriage while I was still in college and seminary. She worked in three different libraries: Wilbur Cross at UConn, the Yale Divinity School Library, and New Haven Public. She taught social studies to help with their tuition when our children were in school. And she worked in their school again when our grandchildren lived with us for several years. She spent years recording, making, and distributing my sermon tapes. She has been my greatest encouragement and fiercest critic in all the places the Lord has taken us. She has regaled our children, grandchildren, and now our great-grands with tales of her family's trips "up north" to the Minnesota lake country when she was young, and fantasy tales full of imaginary creatures that delight young hearts and minds. She enjoys painting and is still speaking occasionally to groups of women. She has a servant's heart and an amazing prayer ministry, and I cannot imagine life without her.

Kathy

Our eldest daughter, Katherine Howe Evans, has a master's degree in counseling, and she earned her doctorate in Education with studies in Oxford and Rome. (We actually roomed together and had one class together during one year in Oxford.) She has been a teacher and a school principal. She is currently the Director of Religious Education for St. Mary's Roman Catholic Church, a very large church about 30 minutes down the road from where Karen and I live in Virginia. Kathy is married to Navy Commander Mike Evans, a Physicians' Assistant who oversees the clinics at the Quantico Marine base. Mike is preparing to become a Deacon in the Roman Catholic Church, and Kathy and Mike are both studying theology. Together they have five children: Hunter, Ryan, and Holly from Mike's first marriage, and Melissa and Joshua from Kathy's, and five grandchildren (so far). All of the Evanses live in Northern Virginia, and it is a delight to spend time with them.

John

Our son John has spent most of his adult life working for different pizza chains, and twice he won the competition for the world's fastest pizza maker.[102] He is now on the management team for the rapidly growing Marco's Pizza chain. John is married to Tracy, the long-time City Clerk of Clermont, Florida. John and

---

[102] You can google his appearance on Regis and Kelly demonstrating his prowess.

Tracy have a six-year-old daughter, Cassidy, who loves all things in nearby Disney, especially the many princesses. The Jr. Howes and John's two older children, Johnny and Madi - just married this year to Johnathan – all live in Central Florida.

<u>Jessica</u>

Our youngest, Jessica Howe Jones, is the Archdeacon of the Gulf Atlantic Diocese of the Anglican Church in North America. She was ordained by my friend and former associate, Neil Lebhar, who invited me to join him in the laying-on of hands. Jess is married to Bruce, CEO of Vicar's Landing, a retirement community in Ponte Vedra, just south of Jacksonville, Florida. The Joneses have two children, Hannah, a sophomore at the University of North Florida, and "D.B." (Donald Bruce VIII), a sophomore in high school. Jess recently completed her second doctorate, the first in worship and this latest in educational theory. The Joneses live about thirty minutes from our condo in Orange Park.

Karen and I give thanks every day for the wonderful family God has given us, and for the opportunity to spend significant time with all of them. One of our greatest blessings is that all of our kids know, love, and follow Jesus. I pray that this sharing of my story may help others do so as well.

To God be the glory, great things he has done!

Appendix A

Louis Howe's Feldspar Mine

An unsigned article on the Internet said this about my grandfather's mine:

George Andrews opened the Howe No. 1 quarry in a granite pegmatite about 1870. Several years later the northern half of the pegmatite was sold to Joshua and William P. Husband and the southern half was leased for 20 years to Charles Hall. In 1905 Louis W. Howe of South Glastonbury acquired both parts of the property and produced 65,000-70,000 tons of feldspar between 1905 and 1928, when it became inactive. The opencut trending N. 5° E ended up being about 100 feet wide, almost 800 feet long, and 100 feet deep at the south end. For a time, it was the largest pegmatite quarry in Connecticut. The feldspar was sold for use in porcelain and for Bon Ami scouring compound. In the early 1990s Vespa Stone Products attempted to use some of the dump material for crushed stone, but too much mica made this unacceptable for construction.

Appendix B

Grandma Jessie Howe's Long Island Clam Chowder

Ingredients

8 quarts quahog clams
8 slices salt pork (1/4 pound)
18 medium potatoes (peeled and chopped)
8 medium onions (chopped)

Instructions

Cut salt pork into pieces, fry until lightly browned.
Steam claims in 3" of water until they open.
Chop well and *save juice.*
Add potatoes & onions to cooked salt pork.
Add water to cover & simmer vegetables until done.
Add clam juice and clams. Cook until tender.
Season with salt & pepper to taste.
Have heavy cream at the table for those who want it.

Serves eight. (Two or three bowls each!) You will be glad I included this.

Appendix C

A Brief History of Trinity School for Ministry
(From TSM's website)
Reprinted with Permission from
Trinity School of Ministry

Trinity School for Ministry is an evangelical seminary in the Anglican tradition. In this fractured world, we desire to be a global center for Christian formation, producing outstanding leaders who can plant, renew, and grow churches that make disciples of Jesus Christ. To this end we are forming Christian leaders for mission.

Trinity School for Ministry was born in the renewal movement of the 1970s. In 1975, the Rt. Rev. Alfred Stanway, a retired Australian missionary bishop, answered a call from members of the Fellowship of Witness to be Trinity's first Dean and President. He moved to the Pittsburgh area and set up an office in his home, using his garage for the library. Bishop Stanway had been recommended by John Stott, J.I. Packer, John Guest, and other evangelical leaders for his vision of renewal and his extraordinary ability to translate this vision into a lively Christian body. He called the Rev. Dr. John Rodgers, a professor and chaplain at Virginia Theological Seminary, to be the senior professor.

Classes began in 1976 with a small faculty and seventeen students—none with sponsoring bishops—meeting in rented classrooms at a local college. Two years later, the seminary purchased an empty Presbyterian Church in Ambridge, PA and the abandoned supermarket across the street. These buildings were then converted into a campus.

Trinity has grown steadily in our residential, online, and partnership programs. Trinity alumni, both lay and ordained, serve both domestically and around the world. We now have a faculty of fourteen and numerous adjunct professors.

Our student body continues to increase, more and more bishops are ordaining Trinity graduates, and the seminary has received millions of dollars in gifts from a growing number of parishes and individuals. Trinity has had many alumni and former members of the faculty who have served as bishops and other significant leadership roles in the Anglican global world. In 2010, the Most Rev. Hector "Tito" Zavala was elected as the Primate of the Southern Cone, making him the first Trinity graduate to oversee a province of the Anglican Communion.

The Rev. Dr. Henry L. Thompson III (Laurie) served as the seventh Dean/President. He stepped down after graduation in May 2022. The Trinity School for Ministry Board of Trustees is pleased to announce the appointment of The Rev. Cn. Dr. Bryan C. Hollon, Ph.D., as the eighth Dean President.

[Note: shortly before going to press TSM changed its name to Trinity Anglican Seminary.]

Appendix D

The Stones Cry Out

A prophecy given in Canterbury Cathedral during the final eucharist of the Leaders' Conference, during the Anglican International Conference on Spiritual Renewal, July 13, 1978. It is set in blank verse, as it was in the monograph, A New Canterbury Tale, Michael Harper, editor, Grove Books, Bramcote Notts, 1978, p. 30-31, reprinted with permission.

Within this mighty edifice –
the stones cry out.
The stones beneath your feet cry out;
The stones beside you cry to heaven,
And these that soar to heaven cry out too.
The stones cry out – of glory and of shame.
They cry out – of time when cloud and fire
From God on high came down
And filled this place.
And some saw that and some saw not.
Some had their lives transformed;
Some went on and plodded on the way
And saw no vision of night or day.
To take them in the new and living way
Which called them on.
These stones cry out – have always cried
In thousand years of love, grace, power
And of the great consuming fire of God.
But this I say to thee –
That I have greater things to make
Than this great building.
I have a living work to do

With stones that live –
In infinite and gracious detail
In the quarry of my heart.
I look upon the stones that I have made,
And they are wayward stones.
From their surface chisel oft
Has glanced aside
And that which I did purpose has been marred;
And yet I stoop again with broken tool
To take the stone that I have made
And work again upon that stone,
That it may be as I have
Long desired it should be.
Each stone is still a living crucible,
And in the inmost heart
There dwells a truth and richness
And a glory infinite. And I do long
That thou shalt not escape the fire
That heats that crucible
Until the dross of foolishness
And pride
And all that does so mar
That work that I have planned
Is driven away.
That which comes from me
Can burst clean out
Upon a long-expectant world'
Who look for glory and fire,
For sacrifice and love and peace
Beyond all human understanding.
I love each stone –
Each stone you are,
Each stone you love;
Each stone in every place from which you come.

I love each stone
And as the fire heats up the crucible,
I know that feel;
I've been through that,
And infinitely more for thee.
I know what thy weak and sinful soul
Can bear. I will not take thee
Through that which thou canst not with me
Outdistance in the world.
I do this to you, child
Because I love thee so –
Because the thing that you do treasure,
Precious in your heart,
Is such a small weak and useless
Counterfeit of that
Deep, pure and lovely purity
That I have stored for thee.
Can you begin to see
That what I do in love
I do in pain unto myself
Because I love thee so?
I would have thee
Let go all life
From thy outstretched hands
Into the hand of God
And into the love of Christ
And into the new empowering grave
Of the Spirit's love within thee.
You are few
Within this earthly tabernacle here.
Yet you are linked
In countless myriads
Gone, and still to come
In my eternal timeless love.
Reach out your hands

Dear children of my heart, just now.
And let these stones cry out
Of what the living stones must be,
And long that that which is of glory,
Pure, astringent, purified
May come down
And straighten up your back
And ennoble all your heart
And take you out
That you may truly
High exalt the Savior's name.

Appendix E

Resolution of the 69th General Convention of the Episcopal Church (1988)

All human life is sacred. Hence, it is sacred from its inception until death. The Church takes seriously its obligation to help form the consciences of its members concerning this sacredness. Human life, therefore, should be initiated only advisedly and in full accord with this understanding of the power to conceive and give birth which is bestowed by God.

It is the responsibility of our congregations to assist their members in becoming informed concerning the spiritual, physiological and psychological aspects of sex and sexuality.

The Book of Common Prayer affirms that "the birth of a child is a joyous and solemn occasion in the life of a family. It is also an occasion for rejoicing in the Christian community" (p 440). As Christians we also affirm responsible family planning.

We regard all abortion as having a tragic dimension, calling for the concern and compassion of all the Christian community.

While we acknowledge that in this country it is the legal right of every woman to have a medically safe abortion, as Christians we believe strongly that if this right is exercised, it should be used only in extreme situations. We emphatically oppose abortion as a means of birth control, family planning, sex selection, or any reason of mere convenience.

In those cases where an abortion is being considered, members of this Church are urged to seek the dictates of their consciences in prayer, to seek the advice and counsel of members of the Christian community and where appropriate the sacramental life of this Church.

Whenever members of this Church are consulted with regard to a problem pregnancy, they are to explore, with grave seriousness, with the person or persons seeking advice and counsel, as alternatives to abortion, other positive courses of action, including, but not limited to, the following possibilities: the parents raising the child; another family member raising the child; making the child available for adoption.

It is the responsibility of members of this Church, especially the clergy, to become aware of local agencies and resources which will assist those faced with problem pregnancies.

We believe that legislation concerning abortions will not address the root of the problem. We therefore express our deep conviction that any proposed legislation on the part of national or state governments regarding abortions must take special care to see that individual conscience is respected, and that the responsibility of individuals to reach informed decisions in this matter is acknowledged and honored.

Made in the USA
Middletown, DE
21 July 2024